Praise for
Good Idea. Now What?

"Getting from step 0 to step 1 is often the hardest part, and Charles understands that. This book lays out a comprehensive strategy that skillfully maps out how to move ideas into that next stage of creation, which will be helpful for any leader."

—**Ben Keesey**
CEO of Invisible Children

"In this approachable, pragmatic book, Charles presents us with a fresh, thoughtful approach of how to get our ideas into the world, while also providing critical perspective on the implications of new ideas on the entrepreneur's often overlooked personal life. Read this before you launch your next project."

—**Dave Blanchard**
Founder of Praxis;
Former IDEO Principal Designer

"Structure and process that powers creatives! Charles T. Lee has penned a witty, inspirational, and approachable manual for both aspiring and veteran entrepreneurs that focuses on turning ideas into strategic execution. Take Nike's advice and 'Just Do It'!"

—**Wade Kawasaki**
Executive Vice President of Coker Group

"People often approach me for advice on making their 'new idea' reality. They usually ask for help via a short e-mail or a quick conversation. The truth is there is so much more to idea making than what can be communicated through a simple response. Having a resource like *Good Idea. Now What?* will help me point people to a practical guide that helps them get on a path that marries their passion with a plan."

—**Tyler Merrick**
Founder and Social Capitalist of Project7

"Thomas Edison (not Albert Einstein) rightly stated that 'Genius is one percent inspiration, 99 percent perspiration.' While you're on your own for the 1 percent, Charles T. Lee's *Good Idea. Now What?* takes you through the 99 percent. Lee's book is light-hearted and witty, but also a sincere read that offers solid business insights, essential for any idea to take flight. If you have a passion to take your idea to market, then *Good Idea. Now What?* will make sure that you are well equipped for the climb."

—**Keith Kall**
Senior Director, Corporate Partnerships for World Vision

"For many creatives and change makers the road isn't always clear, but what Charles has done through *Good Idea. Now What?* is to boil down the vital steps around idea generation, branding, collaboration, and putting first things first—in order to help us chart our course to move the best ideas forward."

—**Jeff Slobotski**
Founder of Silicon Prairie News

"Tired of your ideas limping along? Lost and don't know where to start? Does your world changing idea demand a big dose of momentum and practicality? Charles T. Lee delivers it all in his inspiring book, *Good Idea. Now What?*"

—**Mike Foster**
Creative Principal and Cofounder of PlainJoe Studios

"Charles T. Lee has penned a guide to the hard work of birthing an idea into life. If you read this book, your idea will have an exponentially greater chance of seeing the light of day. Read it."

—**Jeff Shinabarger**
Founder of Plywood People

"With driving clarity, Charles T. Lee helps us cut through the clutter of good intentions and get to work. This book will not only catalyze action, it will lead you to create transformation."

—**Bethany Hoang**
Director of the IJM Institute

"*Good Idea. Now What?* is a great handbook to navigate the chaos of creativity! I love Charles. You'll delight in his practical insights forged in the furnace of his own ideation!"

—**Dave Gibbons**
CEO of XEALOT
Author of *XEALOTS: Defying the Gravity of Normality*

"Charles T. Lee is one of the best idea guys I know. Better than good ideas are ideas that lead to impact—a hallmark of Charles' life. Charles' new book, *Good Idea. Now What?* is a hands-on resource that will serve you as an idea coach helping you to move your great ideas to implementation and finally to major impact!"

—**Greg Ligon**
Vice President and Publisher of Leadership Network

"For many creatives and change makers the road isn't always clear, but what Charles has done through *Good Idea. Now What?* is more than just a book— it's an opportunity to make something. Through proven insights and principles, Charles T. Lee offers you everything you need to turn ideas into realities. All you have to do is follow along."

—**Scott McClellan**
Editor for *Collide* Magazine
Director of ECHO Conference

"Our current world is in desperate need of doers. Men and women who dream big and see that dream come to life—and that's where this book comes in play. Charles is a doer; this book proves that. Well done Charles, thanks for sharing your ideas!"

—**Chris Marlow**
CEO and Founder of Help End Local Poverty

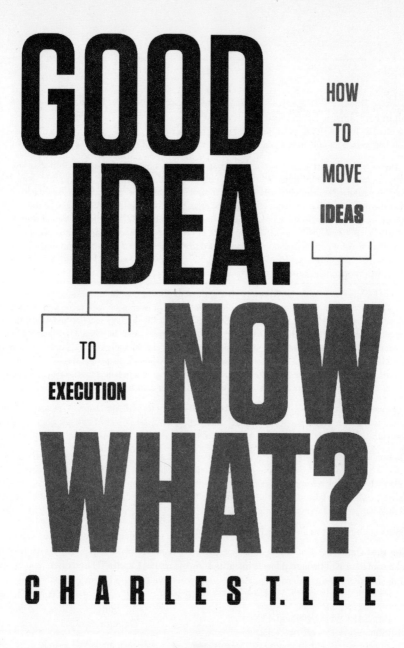

GOOD IDEA. NOW WHAT?

HOW TO MOVE IDEAS

TO EXECUTION

CHARLES T. LEE

WILEY

JOHN WILEY & SONS, INC.

Published by John Wiley & Sons, Inc., Hoboken, New Jersey.
Published simultaneously in Canada.

For general information on our other products and services or for technical support, please contact our Customer Care Department within the United States at (800) 762-2974, outside the United States at (317) 572-3993 or fax (317) 572-4002.

Wiley publishes in a variety of print and electronic formats and by print-on-demand. Some material included with standard print versions of this book may not be included in e-books or in print-on-demand. If this book refers to media such as a CD or DVD that is not included in the version you purchased, you may download this material at http://booksupport.wiley.com. For more information about Wiley products, visit www.wiley.com.

Library of Congress Cataloging-in-Publication Data:

Lee, Charles, 1972-
  Good Idea. Now What? : How to move ideas to execution / Charles T. Lee.
    p. cm.
  ISBN: 978-1-118-16399-3 (hardback : acid-free paper)
  ISBN: 978-1-118-23000-8 (ebk)
  ISBN: 978-1-118-22991-0 (ebk)
  ISBN: 978-1-118-22617-9 (ebk)
    1. Creative ability in business—Management.   2. Creative ability—Management.
3. Entrepreneurship. 4. Strategic planning.   I. Title.

  HD53.L436   2012
  658.4'094—dc23   2011038804

Printed in the United States of America
10 9 8 7 6 5 4 3 2 1

For Tina,
my love & best friend.
For Jonathan & Alexis,
my inspiration & hope.

CONTENTS

PREFACE

Born into a Legacy of Idea Makers

My parents were born during the infancy of the Korean Conflict, a civil war that devastated our small, developing country in Asia. Our postwar Korea was literally in ruins, and the economy was a shambles. There were an estimated 2 million casualties as a result of the war, and thousands of family members were displaced, separated from loved ones on both sides of the border. The environment was one filled with deep grief, anger, and hopelessness.

Fortunately for Korea, the children born during this time—the generation of my parents—refused to let their circumstances get in the way of their efforts to turn their country around. They chose resilience, an unparalleled work ethic, and a "we can't fail" attitude that has helped Korea catapult itself into the top 15 ranking for gross domestic product (GDP). Unbelievable!

When it comes to implementing ideas well, my parents' generation has always been a great source of inspiration for me. Many of them traveled the world to provide new opportunities for their children, as well as develop strong credibility for their homeland. Family and country have always been a source of great pride for my parents' generation. Barriers such as language, education, and discrimination were no match for their unwavering belief that sacrificing for future generations was a privileged responsibility.

They took their ideas and found a way to make them reality.

My heroes. My heritage. My passion.

ACKNOWLEDGMENTS

Good Idea. Now What? was a team effort. It would not have been possible to complete without the help of many great friends and family members. First and foremost, my beautiful wife, Tina, who never ceased to believe in me and supported me throughout the entire process. My kids, Jonathan and Alexis, who allowed Daddy to take some time away from family to write. Bill Denzel, my longtime friend and now agent, who gave me great advice about writing and took the time to walk me into this new world of publishing. The cultural influencers who agreed to be interviewed by me for the book—in the midst of their busy lives—for their friendship and shared passion to help ideas come to life. Sarah Schick, for organizing my life and making sure I had time to work on this book. The team at Ideation who covered me and allowed me to pursue this project in the midst of all of our client work. Dan Ambrosio and the team at John Wiley & Sons, Inc., who saw potential and approached me about the book project. My family of friends (you know who you are!) who have invested in my life with much needed love, encouragement, and perspective. Last, the countless people I have been privileged to interact with over the years about idea making via blogs, projects, and conferences. I'll forever be grateful for all of your input in my life!

INTRODUCTION

Idea Lovers versus Idea Makers

I deas are sexy.

They are attractive, unbridled, and full of inspired passion.

We want to platform them, tell their story, and introduce them to as many people as possible.

Most of us *love* ideas and fall for them quickly and regularly. We are idea lovers! This is probably the reason you picked up this book.

There's no need to apologize here.

Ideas are great. I love ideas. Ideas are what move our world into its future.

Unfortunately, many who have good ideas will never see their ideas come to life. They will actually end up taking their ideas to the grave (literally!). Whether it was a brilliant idea for a business, organization, or personal fulfillment, their ideas will never see the light of day. Tragic.

These individuals are lovers of ideas, not makers of ideas. You see, all idea makers love ideas, but not all idea lovers make ideas come to life. Unlike idea lovers, idea makers are not satisfied with just having a great idea. They are committed to seeing their concepts actualized in the real world. In addition, they are willing to reframe their lives so that their ideas can be implemented well.

Who Is This Book For?

I wrote this book for two kinds of people:

1. The idea lover who is sick of just sitting on great ideas: These are individuals who recognize that their ideas may never come to pass without a strategic process and a developed skill set.

2. The idea maker who needs to refresh and reaffirm his or her understanding of the elements for implementing ideas well: No matter how experienced you may be, this book will be a good resource for sparking meaningful conversations about your ideas.

Whether you are starting a new venture or recalibrating an established work, *Good Idea. Now What?* is designed to be extremely practical. In addition, this book will serve as a springboard for further idea exploration and refinement. You will find numerous recommendations of other resources that will be of great help to your endeavors as an idea maker.

How Does This Book Work?

The format of this book was designed to be engaging at multiple levels and provide ample opportunities for productivity:

- **Parts:** These are the large sections of the book that contain chapters focused around a common theme. I recommend that you do a quick skim of these parts in the Contents each time you pick up the book. This will give you a bird's-eye view of the overall direction and provide context for each collection of chapters.

- **Chapters:** Each of the chapters was designed to stand alone. In other words, you can open up to any chapter and dive right in, without having to go back and read the content prior to that specific point. Although it would be best to start from the beginning to get the full experience, I recognize that some, given their context, may jump straight to a section they perceive to be the most helpful and needed. You'll notice the chapters are brief as well. I wanted this book to be flexible and bite-sized enough for busy individuals and busy teams. Thus, the chapters are purposely short and distinct enough for you to read on the go or together as a group during a staff meeting. (I told you it was practical!)

- ***Good Idea. Now What?*** At the end of each chapter, I've provided some space for you to work through your ideas about the topics covered in the reading. Under "Good Idea," you'll notice that I've highlighted some key thoughts from the chapter to refresh your memory and stir new ideas. You're encouraged to add your own notes for takeaway. The "Now What?" section provides space for you to jot down your next action steps. Always try to be as specific as possible when you work on this section. I encourage you to include details such as dates for follow-up, names of people to connect with, visualization of an idea or process, and so forth. It's your space. Use it!

- **"Taking It Further":** This is a section at the end of each major part created to provide some practical ideas and suggestions to help you take your concepts further. I think you'll enjoy pausing after each large section to process the ideas by yourself or with a group.

This book was not designed for you to simply read and pass along. I'm hoping that some of your thoughts will end up on the pages of this book (or at least on the pages of a corresponding Moleskine journal). I want this book to be functional—something you carry around as you seek to implement your ideas. View it as an idea journal. May it document the evolution of your next great concept!

The Business of Good Ideas

Every good idea needs strong business philosophy and strategy in order to take flight and scale. Although not every idea becomes a business, there are still timeless business principles that can bring much-needed infrastructure, strategy, and perspective for anyone desiring to implement well. This is why I've integrated several business development insights throughout the book to help the idea maker implement his or her idea with good business sense. Creative ideas and the best practices of business should go hand in hand. (You can thank me later!)

A Conversation over Coffee

This book is written to carry the tone and feel of two friends talking about ideas over coffee. It is intentionally informal, uninhibited, and filled with dry humor (or attempts at humor, at least). I wrote in this manner because I think it allows us to be more honest in engaging these important and sometimes complex topics without faking expertise. The truth is that we're all learning and refining along the way.

So sit down with this book and a cup of coffee and enjoy some insights from a friend. And since we're now in conversation, please send any thoughts or questions you may have about the content directly to my personal e-mail: charles@TheIdeation.com (yes, it's real) or use the book's hashtag on Twitter: #GoodIdeaBook. I'll do my best to promptly respond whenever possible. Just don't add me to any e-mail lists that I have not subscribed to, especially since I'm your friend now!

I'm grateful that you've picked up this book, and I look forward to chatting with you in the chapters to come.

—**Charles T. Lee**
www.CharlesTLee.com
@CharlesTLee
#GoodIdeaBook

Where Do Good Ideas Come From?

CHAPTER

1

Strategy or Chance?

"It's about strategy! Be intentional."

"It's about timing and chance! Pray for luck."

How does a good idea come to life? Strategy? Timing? Luck? Yes.

A good idea is often a thought conceived at the intersection of strategy and chance.

Louis Pasteur, a nineteenth-century French scientist and the inventor of the process of pasteurization, said it this way: "Chance favors the prepared mind." In other words, a mind that is trained to engage new ideas is far more likely to recognize important idea connections than the casual observer.

Want to stack the odds in your favor? Here's a little secret that the most effective idea makers use to their advantage: a good grasp of the former—intentional strategy—can actually increase your odds when it comes to the latter—the favor of chance.

Although none of us can control or predict these chance opportunities, we can work toward developing a mind-set and process that allows us to be more proactive toward making our ideas come to life. Our eyes should be focused on the hard work of executing ideas rather than being distracted by the flash of chance. Unfortunately, far too many people over-exert themselves in finding the right opportunity to gain exposure for their idea without giving enough attention to the core business of what they hope to produce. This often comes back to bite them.

History has shown us repeatedly that it takes intentional time and effort to develop a good idea. Even in our age of instant access to information and resources, ideas of significance (even digital ones) are rarely formulated in a quick moment. Although it's true that technology allows us to speed up production, technology still lacks the ability to make intuitive decisions that are often needed to create viable connections between concepts. That's good news! The world still needs creative idea people like you.

But should you rely on chance? I suppose that you could just go for it and hope for the best. Maybe you'll win the lottery as well! (Or not.)

Keep reading.

We all need guiding principles and processes for idea making that allow us to have a prepared mind when chance shows up at the door.

Good Idea (key thoughts from this section)	Now What? (your ideas and next steps for execution)
"Chance favors the prepared mind."	_____
	_____
	_____
Our eyes should be focused on the hard work of executing ideas rather than being distracted by the flash of chance.	_____
	_____
It takes intentional time and effort to develop a good idea.	_____
	_____

Ideas in the Midst

Why do we feel more connected to some ideas than to others?

In a culture that longs for real connectivity, ideas aren't just impersonal concepts that end up as products on a shelf. We consume in hopes of satisfying our intangible desires for fulfillment and joy in life. A good idea is something people want to connect with at a deep level.

Without getting into a debate about what constitutes a good idea, I'd like to share why physical environment and close proximity are significant to the idea-making process, especially as it relates to connecting with the hearts of people.

To their loss, many undermine the importance of *where* an idea is formed. The physical space that surrounds us fuels our creativity and enhances our ability to see and feel what it is we are trying to form. This doesn't mean that we have to be in the coolest space to create, but rather, we must be mindful of pursuing the kind of space that will position our physical bodies toward receiving the best and most relevant experiences related to our passions.

For example, if your passion is to serve the economically poor of your city, developing ideas in a corporate boardroom is probably not the best place to start. Being and living in the environment of those you hope to serve must be the first step of developing an idea. The most creative concepts can be found right in the environments where they will provide the greatest benefit. Who are the stakeholders and main beneficiaries of your passion? Go to them. Listen, learn, love, and take notes.

Most great ideas are rooted in people—not in idealistic theories.

The closer you can get to moving the pendulum of language from *them* to *us* through spatial presence and proximity, the better chance you'll have of actually coming up with ideas that work.

Wisdom from the Streets

Ventura is a beautiful beach city just north of Los Angeles. It is an eclectic community with beautiful, historic architecture and unbelievable weather. It was also the long-time home of one of my closest friends, Greg Russinger, who I met back in the 1990s while playing music in Southern California. We eventually formed a band together with some mutual friends and had an amazing time traveling and performing. For us as twenty-somethings, the sky was the limit and adventure was preferred over any kind of compensation or stability. With Greg as our leader, all of us in the band lived out his spirit of adventure and love of life.

One of the things I admire most about Greg, outside of his incredible love for music, is his genuine care for humanity. Way before it was cool to have a cause, Greg regularly engaged people in his city to bring relief to those in need. It was not uncommon to see him go out of his way to extend hospitality and care for people who were regularly overlooked or ignored by many of us in society. He has an uncanny ability to see people beyond their exterior. One's physical or mental condition was never an obstacle to Greg's engagement. Greg authentically values human life. No strings attached.

One day, while talking with T-Bone, one of his friends who lived on the streets of Ventura, Greg asked him a simple question: "Is there anything I can do to help you with your day-to-day needs?" T-Bone looked at him and responded with two simple words: "Clean clothes." He continued to explain to Greg that the simple reality of clean clothes not only would provide hygienic benefits but would also change the way others would view and interact with him. Clean clothes would remove barriers to human interaction as well as strengthen self-esteem for someone who many considered hopeless.

This insight inspired Greg to create something called Laundry Love. He asked his community of friends to join him in getting clean clothes to the poor or working poor. Greg approached a local Laundromat and asked them for permission to allow him and a group of his friends to come in and sponsor washes for those living under the poverty line. This simple idea allowed for natural relationships to build between people coming to the Laundromat. While in conversations during these free laundry nights,

Greg and his team began to identify the actual needs of their neighborhood and then proceeded to find ways to serve the people accordingly.

Laundry Love soon gained momentum in Ventura, as well as surrounding cities in Southern California. Greg soon invited me to help him establish a nonprofit organization that would help create these kinds of practical ideas to better our world. I gladly joined his efforts and we formed an organization called JustOne (www.Just4One.org). Our goal was—and still is—to create these kinds of everyday ideas for human care.

Initiatives like Laundry Love have continued to grow in these past five years of our organization's existence. Laundry Love now exists in more than 120 locations and serves more than 30,000 people every month via various contextualized services, including basic medical care, job placement, tutoring, haircuts, holiday parties, and food giveaways. And it all started with T-Bone's two-word answer.

I'm a firm believer that the best ideas come from the streets (i.e., the people who will most benefit from the concept). There's something powerful about spending time in the actual environment of the people you hope to reach with your product or service. Unfortunately, many are developing products or services behind closed doors in artificial environments that are disconnected from reality. Start in the space you want to have an impact on. Listen to the very ones you hope to serve.

If you are creating a product for small companies, it is well worth your time to regularly interact with small-business owners. You can attend network meetings, do one-on-one interviews, facilitate focus groups, research pertinent data, and so forth. If you're creating a nonprofit organization that serves orphans in China, you may want to spend some significant time overseas developing the business plan while meeting with orphanages in existence, state officials, potential sponsors, and people who are knowledgeable in this area. I know this sounds basic and is just common sense, but I can't tell you how many times start-ups have overlooked this truth for developing a viable idea. If you don't start on the so-called streets, you may end up developing things for people who don't even exist.

Spatial Distance?

Are there times to move away to reflect upon the environment you hope to serve? Absolutely! Spatial distance can actually bring clarity to concepts and produce a lot of good. I'm simply making the case that you should, if possible, start in the same space as the people you hope will benefit from your concepts. I've found this to be true for businesses, organizations, and movements.

Spatial interaction is also cyclical. We need regular times on the inside as well as on the outside of the world we are trying to serve. Proximity and distance are both your greatest assets and your greatest hindrances to idea formation. I read a book a few years back by Larry Bossidy and Ram Charan called *Execution: The Discipline of Getting Things Done* that followed the stories of several chief executive officers (CEOs) of major Fortune 500 companies who were getting laid off in the 1980s and 1990s. Surprisingly, their dismissals were often rooted in their disconnection with lower-tier employees. Many of them were so used to interacting with only C-level executives that they lost touch with the very people who ultimately produced the day-to-day success of their respective companies. This relational distance created ideas and processes that just didn't work.

One of my favorite TV shows, *Undercover Boss*, further highlights this truth. In this show, CEOs of significant companies go undercover, disguising themselves as entry-level employees, in hopes of discovering what really goes on at the ground level. CEOs who participate usually walk away with a new perspective and a deeper appreciation for how hard their employees work—at all levels of their companies.

If you want to create or develop an idea, stay close to the people who will benefit the most and live in the environment in which the innovation will take place.

Good Idea (key thoughts from this section)	Now What? (your ideas and next steps for execution)
Who are the stakeholders and main beneficiaries of your passion? Go to them. Listen, learn, love, and take notes.	
Proximity and distance are both your greatest assets and your greatest hindrances to idea formation.	*a reason why our leaders also need to be serving.

Is there a
Need for a better way
to clean? *yes!*

- Health, Safety
- Time
- #
- pollution

CHAPTER

3

My Need for Need

why do you need to
learn Algebra?
- sp gifts?

God's plan

ost people learn best when they sense a need to learn. Forced learning rarely works. It may develop a certain level of discipline, but true learning requires active participation. Most adults don't become proactive until they get to a place of needing to solve a problem. For example, how many people seek counseling before they experience a crisis?

Unfortunately, many leaders of companies or organizations have ceased to view innovation as a need. They have settled for expertise instead. More specifically, they have settled for static expertise from 10 years ago! This lack of need is killing thousands of companies and organizations. Disguising this organizational commitment to death with management nomenclature or faulty rationalization based on excuses such as limited resources and time will not prevent the inevitable.

Shift happens. But you can make it happen for your business or organization in a way that allows it to flourish into its future. Here are some ideas for architecting a culture of need:

- **Create space for the unfamiliar.** Take yourself and your team (if you have one) to unfamiliar spaces that will heighten your need to engage new ideas. Consider participating or attending an event outside the scope of your usual professional expertise. This will often spark unexpected creativity.

- **Revisit and re-identify what you're trying to solve.** Regularly go back and reconsider why you're producing what you're producing. This may sound elementary, but it's important. This takes on the spirit of what legendary coaches like Vince Lombardi and John Wooden would do with their players each year: reintroduce them to their respective sports. Ask your team why they do what they do. And if you dare, ask them why they think *you* do what you do.

- **Humble yourself and invite the third eye.** None of us have arrived. Period. All of us need help, even those of us who are considered experts in the field. For most of us, we are too close to the action to see what's going on around us. We need outside eyes and voices to help form the future of our companies or organizations. Even as a consultant myself, I need other consultants and coaches. The reality is that all of us are faking it to some level. Just admit it. We all could use some help. Take the time and resources to invest in your work. Outside voices will save you thousands of dollars as well as countless moments of unnecessary heartache.

Innovation requires a deep sense of learning that is rooted in a deep sense of need. Do you feel the need for anything?

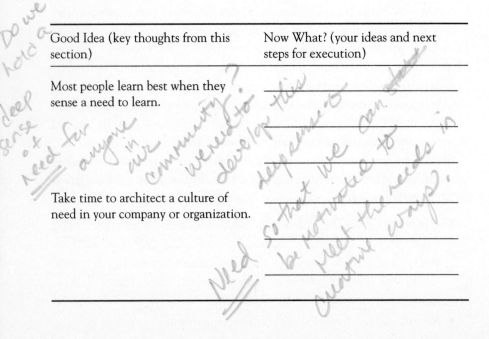

Good Idea (key thoughts from this section)	Now What? (your ideas and next steps for execution)
Most people learn best when they sense a need to learn.	
Take time to architect a culture of need in your company or organization.	

(handwritten annotations surrounding the table:) Do we hold a deep sense of need for anyone in our community? We need to develop this deep sense so that we can be motivated to meet the needs in creative ways. Need

CHAPTER

4

Medici Changed My Life

Creative ideas are often birthed when two or more ideas collide in sweet complementary harmony—kind of like what's depicted in those Reese's Peanut Butter Cups commercials. ("You got your chocolate in my peanut butter!") Few things in life bring more joy to an idea maker than these aha moments. Although many of these creative intersections appear to be spontaneous, unplanned, and based on chance, I posit that you can actually increase the frequency of these magical moments. Let me explain.

Back in the fourteenth century, the House of Medici, a successful political family and eventual owners of the largest bank in Europe, began a movement of intentionally connecting the leading cultural thinkers and shapers of their time. They invested massively to fund and gather creatives, scientists, architects, and business leaders from multiple disciplines. They developed strategic partnerships in cultural efforts and even orchestrated marriages to connect with other elite families. The Medicis believed that the convergence of seemingly unrelated disciplines was key to discovering new ideas and igniting innovation. They wanted to eliminate the unspoken paradigm of their time that ideas should be made in silos. I think the Medicis were well ahead of their time in thinking multidimensional and open source. By the way, many credit the Medicis for developing the roots of that little movement we now call the Renaissance. Want to start a movement?

11

The Medici Tweet?

Doesn't this sound a lot like the opportunity we now have because of the Internet? Consider all of the companies that have been built on the backs of existing work, such as the various social media platforms. Twitter alone has inspired the birth of numerous companies, including TweetDeck, HootSuite, TwitHawk, and many others. In return, these companies have made Twitter more successful by making it easier to use and attracting new users. An interdependence is born, and both parties benefit.

Once you start to think this openly about how ideas are made, it changes what you look for in the process of development. It is no longer about your idea competing with other ideas. Rather, it's more about finding how your idea fits into the bigger world of ideas.

Whenever you come up with a new idea, there's a high probability that it stands on the shoulders of previous thoughts that carried various aspects of your concept. In other words, you didn't pull it out of thin air. Most, if not all, ideas are connected to previous thoughts, even the so-called new ones. Ideas need context, and context requires the existence of previous ideas or thoughts.

Why is this obvious thought so significant and practical? Here's why:

1. It should cause us to never underestimate the creative potential of normal or everyday interaction with ideas. Given the right set of circumstances, with a little bit of nurturing, we will find ourselves in the midst of some of the greatest ideas we will ever have the privilege of experiencing. Living life with this perspective will increase opportunities for creativity. It will create what I call intentionally spontaneous moments for creativity and innovation.

2. In light of number 1, write down or record anything that inspires you and read number 3.

3. Unrelated doesn't necessarily mean unrelated. Don't be too quick to disassociate ideas from one another. Allow ideas to dwell with one another. I used to extensively categorize ideas, but I then came to realize that it actually hindered my creative processing of thoughts. Furthermore, I rarely found myself reviewing the numerous categories of thought I had created in hopes of organizing. It became quite burdensome. Organizing the ideas into just a few thought categories, such as technology, compassion, and business, and then regularly

teaching • ministry • Norwex

cross-pollinating the concepts has worked well for me. I usually go back to ideas I've jotted down about every two weeks. I actually have a reminder on my calendar so I don't forget.

4. In light of the emphasis on cross-pollination just discussed, consider doing something out of the ordinary. This reinforces what we saw in Chapter 3.

5. Since unrelated ideas can come together to produce creative moments, I encourage you to engage in activities outside of your normal rhythm of life. Whether it's taking a class or reading a book unrelated to your field, attending a workshop outside your expertise at a conference, traveling a different route to work, rearranging furniture at home or in your office, or changing where you sit in meetings, slight alterations can make a world of difference in our creative development.

As you establish this kind of openness and praxis in your life, you will begin to experience the exponential growth of your ideas. Enjoy!

Good Idea (key thoughts from this section)	Now What? (your ideas and next steps for execution)
The convergence of seemingly unrelated disciplines is a key to discovering new ideas and igniting innovation.	
It is no longer about your idea competing with other ideas. Rather, it's more about finding how your idea fits into the bigger world of ideas.	*No idea is new anyway!*
It is possible to create intentionally spontaneous moments for creativity and innovation.	*yes — practice — look for it, be ready for it.*

plan an amazing meal

Don't Settle for Good

During my nine-year stint as a college professor, I had the privilege of teaching several high-achieving students who were considered successful by academia. This group included two basic kinds of students:

1. The first kind of student achieved success by working above and beyond the expected workload of the college courses being taken. Many of these students recognized the unique educational opportunity they were in and took full advantage of their access to transformative information.
2. The second kind did just good enough to achieve As in class, often by banking on their ability to deliver last-minute projects that satisfied course requirements. This kind of student usually received the same kind of high honors and accolades from the institution as the first.

To some, what matters most is whether they meet the basic standards of an institution or profession. Many think that being good enough signifies success or a job well done.

Here's the bad news: this is not the way things usually work in the real world. When was the last time you heard of a person achieving success by meeting the minimum standards of his or her profession? When was the last time in this digital age that a product that was considered good enough survived for any extended period of time? Someone will usually create something better to offer.

15

Looking back, I find it unfortunate that the just good enough students cheated themselves of producing their best work. They missed out on experiencing the fullness of their potential. Less-than-great effort skinned with hyped talent and ability may produce outcomes that are good enough, but rarely will it birth the extraordinary—the accomplishments that people remember and talk about. Reaching a standard should never be the goal of our vocational or creative pursuits. The world doesn't eagerly wait for a 70 or 80 percent effort. It longs for our very best. In fact, as Seth Godin often says, "Good is boring." Our work must be remarkable. In other words, our work must cause people to want to share their experiences with their friends and family.

If you're going to do something of passion, do it with all that you are and hope to be. Don't settle for good enough. It will rarely be good enough, and it will shortchange you of the kind of life you were designed to live.

Good Idea (key thoughts from this section)	Now What? (your ideas and next steps for execution)
Less-than-great effort skinned with hyped talent and ability may produce outcomes that are good enough, but rarely will it birth the extraordinary—the accomplishments that people remember and talk about.	*Teaching* *Ministry* *God-Life* *Nurse* *Want people to go home talking*

Taking It Further

Consider your past. What significant ideas has chance provided for you? How were you ready—or not ready—to receive them? How will you align your life today to be ready when new ideas show up?

Where are you currently trying to come up with new ideas? Where and with whom could you spend more time to help bring your idea to life?

Take your team to an unfamiliar environment where they will develop a need to learn (without risking their lives!). For example, have them visit an unfamiliar neighborhood dominated by another culture, volunteer at a local school, participate in acts of charity, sit through an opera, or interview a stranger from a completely different field. Meet later to discuss the experience and brainstorm solutions to a problem you've been trying to solve.

Create an intentionally spontaneous moment for creativity by sitting down with magazines from two diverse fields that inspire and interest you. Quickly flip through the magazines and rip out the pages that interest you. Now look at the two piles together and see what connections you can identify. What new ideas arise?

w/a guarantee!

Life after Inspiration

2

Life after Inspiration

CHAPTER

6

Addicted to Inspiration

All of us need inspiration.

It reminds us of our hopes, dreams, and the kind of life we hope to live. It sparks, fuels, and keeps our creativity alive. But inspiration can also become an addictive drug that causes deep delusion, distraction, and ultimately great harm. It has the power to lure us into unreal expectations that give us a false sense of accomplishment and productivity.

Let's all admit it together: we are inspiration junkies. Most of us long for the latest ideas, news stories, gadgets, apps, links, videos, and conferences because we think these things will give us an extra push or edge over our competition. We want to be in the know. Some of us will disguise this need for inspiration as professional development. Call it whatever you want. The truth is we're hooked.

A culture driven by this need to be constantly inspired is bound to become less interested in the heavy lifting necessary to implement ideas well. It's a whole lot easier (and more enjoyable) to *talk* about ideas than it is to *execute* them.

Unfortunately, the distraction of inspiration is all around us, especially in an age of Google. Ideas that inspire are a dime a dozen. That's cheaper than the dollar bins at Target!

I don't write this to knock the thought of inspiration. As mentioned earlier, we all need it. The problem arises when inspiration itself becomes the goal, the thing we aspire to. Inspiration is a great additive to our work, but it should never become the end of our pursuit. In other words, inspiration is a means to an end and not the end itself. Inspiration often tricks our minds into thinking that we are actually doing something with our idea—when all we are really doing is dreaming or maybe telling someone else about this great new idea. Try to keep in mind that mental advancement in thought should have some corresponding movement in the physical world.

Could it be that many of us are dying of inspiration overload? Here are some suggestions on curbing our addiction to inspiration:

- **Limit new ventures.** As a serial entrepreneur, I have to constantly remind myself that so-called new work must be meaningful and add to what I sense to be my current life direction. This means that a good opportunity that presents itself to me is not necessarily the right opportunity for me. Although we may not always be able to discern the difference between these two, it is still valuable to embed these kinds of thoughts and questions into our minds, especially in seasons when we're launching new projects.

- **Limit your areas of focus.** Working toward refining and pruning our commitments into a few key areas will help us stay focused. Becoming too broad in engagement usually comes at the cost of giving up meaningful specifics. The old saying is true: "There's no such thing as a free lunch." Someone has to pay for it. In other words, doing everything comes with a deep price tag. Don't be known as someone who does everything. Be known as someone who does the right things. Are there areas that you're currently engaging that you really don't need to be a part of? Why not create a strategy to limit involvement?

- **Limit online information intake.** Determine how much time you will spend each day/week in consuming online information and inspiration. We all know that a short excursion online in following a trail of information can often turn minutes into hours. Setting a flexible and realistic guideline for online engagement will allow you to live a more productive and focused life. I have personally set various times throughout the day to engage in online activity. Keeping end times in mind has helped me immensely in making sure I do what matters most.

- **Limit meetings.** You don't need to meet with everyone who asks for a meeting. Don't let your insecurity of letting others down get in the way of living a healthful and productive life. View each unnecessary meeting as precious time away from doing what you were designed to do. How many times after a day of meetings have you thought, "Why does it feel like I haven't accomplished much today?" Unnecessary meetings can and will kill your productivity.

Good Idea (key thoughts from this section)	Now What? (your ideas and next steps for execution)
It's a whole lot easier (and more enjoyable) to *talk* about ideas than it is to *execute* them.	_____ _____ _____
Inspiration is a great additive to our work, but it should never become the end of our pursuit.	_____ _____ _____
Inspiration, or the advancement of your idea in thought, should have some corresponding movement in the physical world.	_____ _____ _____
Don't be known as someone who does everything. Be known as someone who does the right things.	_____ _____ _____

CHAPTER

7

What Plan?

In the realm of ideas, there's no shortage of passion. On the other hand, there appears to be a drought when it comes to the implementation of ideas.

Passion without an actionable plan will eventually end up in the grave—sometimes literally. Consider all of the books that were never written, songs that were never sung, humanitarian efforts that never saw the light of day, and business ideas that have gone to the grave with the very people who thought of these concepts that could have changed lives.

Passion Unrealized

All of this is most definitely easier said than done. Who doesn't want to create effective processes and actionable steps? The problem is that many feel paralyzed when faced with the reality of doing the hard work of research and developing an infrastructure that facilitates a culture of idea making. Effective idea makers are consistently thinking about the how as much as they are considering the what and why. Infrastructure and actionable steps drive their thinking, rather than simply piling on more great ideas.

I can almost hear what some of you are saying right now: "I'm not organized, nor do I even have energy to be!" Unfortunately, that excuse won't work in the real world (unless of course, you're independently wealthy and can hire whomever you want). Okay, back to reality.

Most creatives who live out their dreams have actualized their passion through intentional planning and hard work. Period. So now that *that* excuse is removed, let's plan!

In planning out action for your passion, here are some foundational questions you may want to regularly reflect upon as you move forward in your endeavor:

- Why are you doing what you're doing?
  - o This question gets to the root of your motives and unveils the criteria for *your* success. Are you (or hoping to be) an idea maker so that you can be your own boss? Earn a lot of money? Transition to a new career? Make the world a better place?
  - o Clarifying the why will become a great source of strength and focus during times of difficulty and confusion. Take time to write this down on paper (yes, paper) and place it somewhere that you will be able to see it regularly.
- What are you trying to do, and how will you do it?
  - o The answer to this question provides the nuts and bolts of your endeavor. Yes, it provides you with objectives and process. It's a question that I find myself asking every day with our team. A large vision without tangible objectives and a process will remain wishful thinking.
  - o This is the question that all teams must continually think about. This will force you to create daily, weekly, monthly, and/ or annual metrics for your work. How will you know if you have reached your objectives? Does everyone else on your team know as well? Are your objectives visible, posted prominently some-where in your workspace?
- Whom will you work with?
  - o Finding the right partners and team members is essential to the success of an entrepreneur. Companies/organizations rise and fall because of team dynamics. Never undermine or take for granted the process of hiring or partnering. The future of your company may depend on it. I'll spend more time developing this principle in the latter portion of this book.
  - o The difficulty with finding the right people is that you really need to work with them on a project to learn whether they are the

right fit. Also, don't make hiring or partnering decisions solely based on friendship. Friendship alone is not the answer to creating good business partnerships. I recommend that you engage smaller project opportunities with the people you hope to work with before committing to greater partnership. This will save you a lot of heartache in the long run!

Taking time to regularly ask yourself the preceding questions will keep you on track and make the journey a lot more enjoyable.

Good Idea (key thoughts from this section)	Now What? (your ideas and next steps for execution)
Passion without an actionable plan will eventually end up in the grave—sometimes literally.	
Effective idea makers are consistently thinking about the how as much as they are considering the what and why. Infrastructure and actionable steps drive their thinking.	
Most creatives who live out their dreams have actualized their passion through intentional planning and hard work.	
A large vision without tangible objectives and a process will remain wishful thinking.	

CHAPTER 8

Dig a Little Deeper

Every idea needs healthy interrogation and a plan.

The Dreaded Business Plan

A business plan is essential for any endeavor because it provides practical direction for vision and passion. Regardless of style or length, the actual process of writing up a business plan will provide much-needed internal clarity. It's a great exercise in identifying and refining a company's values, processes, and objectives.

Even if you're starting a nonprofit (which, in my opinion, is a horrible label for that field), you will need a business plan. From my experience, many nonprofit start-ups shy away from language like *business, revenue, customers, market audit,* and so on. Get over it. Don't get tripped up by the language of business because you think that it doesn't match your organizational nomenclature. You need to think of it in terms of process. As they say, don't throw out the baby with the bathwater. Remember, there is a precious baby in the bathwater whom you need to care for! Too many good not-for-profit organizations fold due to the lack of a good business model. Fortunately, there are numerous resources[1] that can help you draft a business plan. All it takes is a quick trip to your local bookstore (or Amazon) to get started.

---

[1]Start by visiting www.sba.gov, the website for the U.S. Small Business Administration. They provide helpful guidelines for writing a business plan, as well as several resources for small businesses.

Wisdom from Wade

Wade Kawasaki is one of my go-to friends when it comes to business strategy and development. He is the executive vice president of Coker Group, the parent company of Coker Tire Co., Inc., an industry leader in tires and wheels for antique vehicles. Wade is responsible for Coker's business acquisitions, global distribution and manufacturing structure, and corporate infrastructure. He has consulted for numerous companies and not-for-profit organizations on business governance and infrastructure. Wade is a firm believer that infrastructure creates order and processes to support those who are doing the creative work.

During one of our recent meals together, I asked him for his thoughts on organizational infrastructure, creativity, and development of a strong business. Here are some of the nuggets of wisdom I gained from Wade during our conversation:

- Many creatives create and then backfill their idea with organization. This is reactive at best and, at worst, fatal to their endeavors. Proactive organization is far better than reactive organization.

- Everything is about execution, and a big part of execution is completion. It's not the art of doing, but rather the art of getting things done. Infrastructure and processes can help create a system in which things get done.

- When developing a business plan, don't overlook organizational governance. What do the bylaws and constitution need to look like for the organization to become what you want it to be?

- Create a board that is executive in nature (i.e., a team that is filled with people who get things done and hold others accountable). Too many boards are filled with either the biggest names or major funders who aren't necessarily the ones who get the work done. Although you may need these individuals, try to primarily gather more execution-minded people to build the organization.

- Communication is key! The clearer you are with vision and values, the more flexible you can be with infrastructure. There will be less need for checks and balances along the way when people are clear about where the company is going.

- As you grow, get more specific about each role in the organization. Scale requires clarity regarding performance expectations.

Wade will be the first one to tell you that building a strong company or organization with a robust business plan is a more painful path to take, but in the long run it will be much more rewarding and enjoyable.

A Few Questions for Idea Makers

As you can see from Wade's comments, great ideas need strategic infrastructure and a plan for implementation. Discovering this plan is often the result of healthy questioning. Idea makers whom I have worked with tenaciously assess their ideas on an ongoing basis and invite others to do the same.

The following is a basic list of questions that you may want to ask while working toward implementation or a plan. Yes, "while working" is the key. I've found that some of the best questions arise within the context of moving forward. In other words, there's no way you will have all of the necessary questions or answers prior to working on an idea. Several of the following questions will be further explored in the chapters to come:

- Why/how is your idea unique or important? Will you bring something unique or significant to the table?
- Whom is your idea for? Is there a specific niche of people you're trying to reach?
- Who's in your network, and do they really like your idea? Be honest.
- Why should we care about your idea?
- Is your idea sustainable? How will you fund it and allow it to grow?
- Is your idea scalable? What level of growth would you like to see?
- What is the purpose of your idea, and are you able to share the gist of the concept with someone in less than 15 seconds? Is that brief description compelling enough to attract someone to join you?
- Do you have a written business plan? How often do you revisit it?
- (For viral ideas) Is it reproducible? Can others quickly understand the concept and run with it?
- Who is willing to sacrificially work with you on the idea? Are you willing to give your life for this idea?
- How disciplined are you? Do you have a creative process or method for organization?
- Are you ready to stay up late and do whatever it takes?
- Is your family on board and willing to journey with you?

These kinds of questions should continually be at the forefront of your thinking and guide your planning and implementation. Don't be discouraged if you feel as though you don't have all the answers to these questions right now. Most of them will come as you move forward.

Take the first step. It signifies commitment, which will open many doors that will help you move your idea to execution. As Scottish mountain climber W. H. Murray said:

Until one is committed, there is hesitancy, the chance to draw back, always ineffectiveness. Concerning all acts of initiative and creativity there is one elementary truth, the ignorance of which kills countless ideas and splendid plans: That the moment one definitely commits oneself, then providence moves too.

All sorts of things occur to help one that would never otherwise have occurred. A whole stream of events issues from the decision, raising in one's favor all manner of unforeseen incidents, meetings and material assistance, which no man could have dreamt would have come his way.

Good Idea (key thoughts from this section)	Now What? (your ideas and next steps for execution)
Great ideas invite careful questioning. Great questions often lead to a more intentional strategy and accountability.	
A business plan is essential for any endeavor because it provides practical direction for vision and passion.	
Don't be discouraged if you feel as though you don't have all the answers to your questions right now. Most of them will come as you move forward.	

CHAPTER

9

Ideas Don't Work; You Do!

My family immigrated to New York on June 2, 1978. I still remember the awe of the ride from the airport to my aunt and uncle's home just outside of the city. I was completely blown away at the size of the buildings, the grandeur of the city, and the variety of cars I saw on the road. It far exceeded anything a five-year-old could have imagined from a foreign land.

It got even better when we drove through the neighborhood where my aunt and uncle lived. The houses in the neighborhood were massive (or at least I thought they were in comparison to where we had come from!). They had beautiful lawns and were set in a picturesque background filled with trees and hills. It was breathtaking to say the least.

The home we entered was beautiful as well. When I met my cousins for the first time, I interrupted their viewing of *Heckle and Jeckle*—in color! (Yes, I am that old.)

I thought to myself that living in America was going to be a piece of cake! Just look at all the great things this country offers. Boy, was I wrong!

After a few weeks, our family found a little apartment in Flushing, New York. It was a humble space close enough to the city where my parents had found some employment. I quickly came to grips with the fact that pursuing the American dream was going to be anything but easy. My father would wake me early each morning so that he could take me along as he drove my mother to her garment factory job before dropping me off at school.

Our first family car was an old Pontiac Buick that cost $200 and came with half of the windows intact. We improvised and used Saran wrap to cover up where the other windows were supposed to be. Nevertheless, it was still good to have our own car.

I learned early on that hard work was going to be a hallmark of my life. My parents had no other alternative. As immigrants, they didn't speak English, which meant they didn't have the luxury of stepping into the kinds of white-collar jobs they once had back in Korea. They started their lives over again—at the bottom, with practically nothing. They always told me growing up that opportunities would arise if we committed ourselves to working harder than the rest.

A few years later, my parents got the break they needed with an opportunity to start a restaurant in Los Angeles's Koreatown. They took full advantage of it and worked 16- to 18-hour days as they embarked on their new venture. Slowly but surely, they began to gain momentum and a reputation in the Korean restaurant industry as innovators. My parents produced several trends in Korean restaurants in the 1980s and 1990s that have since become iconic staples in Korean food.

We didn't have much when we started. Most opportunities were out of reach for our family. Nevertheless, my parents' insatiable desire to work hard and make a better life for us ultimately prevailed.

The hard work of idea making requires a deep gut check. You can't use excuses such as, "I don't have enough time" or "I just don't know where to start," as rationalization for not pursuing the kind of life you know you are meant to live. Isn't it amazing how time just shows up when we are given an opportunity to do what we want to do? The truth is that we will *make* time for the things we value.

One of the recent companies I started was primarily built between the hours of 10 PM and 3 AM most weeknights and all day long on Saturdays. Given our financial situation at the time, I knew that I could not drop everything and pursue my passion. Rather, my wife and I decided that I would dedicate two years toward building this company during my off-hours. I regularly found myself heading to my office (a.k.a. the dining table) to work on the business after my wife and kids had gone to bed. I committed myself to devoting three to five hours, four to five times a week, toward developing my dream. I did the math, and the hours added up to over 600 hours a year. I got a lot done, and now I'm living my passion full time.

What could you create with a few hundred extra hours a year? What could you implement if you knew you had the time to remove obstacles to your dream? What's holding you back? What's at stake if you don't do this?

Bootstrapping for Project 7

In 2008, my friend Tyler Merrick started a new kind of company called Project 7. After building a successful pet food business, Tyler decided to focus his attention on creating a company that would produce everyday products such as bottled water, mints, gum, and coffee to benefit seven areas of social need: hunger, illness, peace, homelessness, safe water, environment, and education. Project 7 gives away a large portion of its profits to worthy charities in these seven areas of focus.

Project 7's quick growth in the overall market—evidenced by their products' presence in thousands of retail stores today—may give the impression that they are a large corporation pushing out products with unlimited capital. This is most definitely not the case. It is actually the result of Tyler and his small team choosing to bootstrap to remain efficient. This choice allows Project 7 to accomplish its mission—giving generously to help people in need. Project 7 is a sacrificial work of love to make our world a better place.

Tyler rightly refers to himself as a social capitalist. He recently shared with me some lessons he's learned about scaling an idea or dream well. Here's a list of some of the things he shared during our time together:

- **Moonlight your dreams**. Continue to do what you're doing while you put in extra hours to build your dream on the side. You have to be willing to let a passion be a minor part of your life until you can get to the point where full-time investment becomes essential.

- **Don't overexpose yourself to risk.** It is wrong to think that you have to go all in for a dream to really work. Too many people go all in prematurely, and the resulting discouragement prematurely snuffs out their dreams. Timing is important. Don't be too hasty and give up everything. It takes time to build an idea. You'll know when you are at the intersection of change.

- **Embrace the discipline of trimming.** Trimming must be a constant reality for business owners. Too often, a little success causes our eyes to grow bigger than our bank accounts. It's analogous to a newly-wed couple who decides to buy a four-bedroom house because they both have great jobs. It's nice, but in most cases, unnecessary. As you launch and scale your idea, be sure to filter out whether or not something is a need versus a want. Filter these opportunities for expansion through trusted friends and mentors.

Become a Bootstrapper!

Tyler's story is a common one among people who transition into living their passions. The switch to full-time pursuit rarely happens overnight. Actually, I'm glad it doesn't. There are life and business lessons to be learned by bootstrapping. It's good for the soul. It will also give you perspective once you get there. (By the way, none of us will ever fully get there. Welcome to life. It's all about the journey.)

Good Idea (key thoughts from this section)	Now What? (your ideas and next steps for execution)
You can't use excuses such as, "I don't have enough time" or "I just don't know where to start," as rationalization for not pursuing the kind of life you know you are meant to live.	_____ _____ _____
We will make time for the things we value.	_____ _____ _____
Bootstrapping is the norm for idea makers.	_____ _____ _____

CHAPTER

10

Choose Family

No idea happens in a vacuum. The idea maker's choice to pursue an idea is bound to impact that person's relationships with other people—whether friends, family, or coworkers. For some, the actualization of an idea comes at the great cost of human relationships, even with those they dearly love.

As a child, I saw this up close as my parents took on their entrepreneurial pursuits. Although there were many other relational factors that led to their eventual separation and divorce, there's no doubt that their nonstop working lifestyles hindered them from creating enough space or time to strengthen our family relationships.

Our vacations, when we did have any, were usually last-minute trips from Los Angeles to Las Vegas. In hindsight, I can see why they chose to go to Vegas when they had the chance. Not only was it a place that was within driving distance, but it also allowed them to let off some steam. Due to the nature of their work in the Korean restaurant industry, they were never able to go away for extended periods. Quite honestly, I don't know what my parents would have done *with* time.

Don't get me wrong. I think my parents did the best they could with what they had. I don't blame them. They deeply loved me and did everything in their power to give me opportunities that they themselves never had.

Although my story may feel unfortunate at many levels, I am so thankful for the life lessons I've walked away with in regard to family life, work, and ideas. As you pursue your dreams, consider these thoughts about family:

- They see you for who you really are and still love you.
- Work may come and go, but families are irreplaceable.
- It takes as much work, if not more, to build a family as it does a business.
- Life is much more enjoyable when you can share it with family.
- Family reminds us of why—and for whom—we are ultimately working.

Other idea makers who recognize this have created altered life rhythms so that they may intentionally bring health to the relationships they most dearly care about.

One such example is my good friend Jeff Shinabarger. Jeff is by far one of the most creative young entrepreneurs I know. He lives in Atlanta, Georgia, and leads an innovative network of social entrepreneurs called Plywood People. Plywood People are innovators who seek to solve social problems, both locally and internationally, by organizing, innovating, and managing ideas that produce change. Jeff's imprint and influence can be seen on several projects and campaigns that you may have come across. He's just one of those guys who doesn't feel the need to be on a platform to be fulfilled.

Jeff is also a new father. In recent months, he has worked to shift his priorities and schedule in hopes of building a healthy marriage and family.

I spoke to Jeff recently about the relationship between ideas and family life. He had some great thoughts, including the following:

- It's important not to analyze family success by the success of your ideas.
- One thing I have been thinking about lately is, 'What if my greatest ideas were for my family instead of for others?'
- How come I spend so much energy thinking of ideas for my organization or business when I'm not using that same level of creative energy for my own family? Things like that should have the most level of creativity.

- What do I want to be known for in relation to my own family? If everyone else calls me a creative but my own family doesn't, then I don't think I've lived the full responsibility that I have been given as a dad—I really didn't give them the attention and creative energy that I gave everyone else.
- I want to raise children that are more creative than I am. If I'm not encouraging them in that, I feel like I have really failed as a dad.

Are you serious? There are people who think like this? It was quite humbling to hear this from a 31-year-old.

Stay mindful of those who will stick with you through thick and thin when you're pursuing an idea. Your gain at their loss is no gain to you.

Good Idea (key thoughts from this section)	Now What? (your ideas and next steps for execution)
The idea maker's choice to pursue an idea is bound to impact that person's relationships with other people.	_____ _____ _____
Work may come and go, but families are irreplaceable.	_____ _____
Life is much more enjoyable when you can share it with family.	_____ _____

Taking It Further

Are you addicted to inspiration? How does this addiction show up in your daily life? How do you deal with it?

Plan action for your passion with these questions:

- Why are you doing what you're doing?
- What are you trying to do, and how will you do it?
- Who will you work with?

Regardless of style or length, write a business plan. It will provide much-needed internal clarity as to your values, processes, and objectives. Use the list of questions found in Chapter 8 to prompt your thinking.

What could you create with a few hundred extra hours a year? What's holding you back? What's at stake if you don't do this?

Are you applying the same level of creativity and energy you use for work to strengthen and build up your family life?

Overcoming Creative Resistance

CHAPTER

11

Wipe Your Nos and Buts

No.
   Not yet.
   Of course not!
I have no money.
I have no time.
I have no _____!
But I can't.
But I don't know how!
But what about _____?
But what will they _____?

For every *yes* we can come up with about an idea, I'm sure we can think
of a hundred *nos* and *buts*. The internal and external battles for an idea
can become quite overwhelming. These battles can lead to exhaustion,
discouragement, paralysis, and even the death of an idea. It's definitely
true that when it comes to ideas, only the strong survive.

Does it have to be this way? Are the enemies of our ideas real or
just imagined? Can this creative battle be won? Can "resistance," as
Steven Pressfield wrote about in his wonderful book *The War of Art*,[1]
be overcome?

---

[1]Steven Pressfield, *The War of Art: Break Through the Blocks and Win Your Inner Creative
Battles* (New York: Warner Books, 2003).

A Prehistoric Brain

Seth Godin refers to this instinctive resistance toward ideas as the *Lizard Brain*.[2] It's the physical part of our brain—a prehistoric lump—that is responsible for controlling our fears, rage, and reproductive drive. It kicks in whenever we sense change, possible accomplishment, or risk. Pressfield refers to it as the voice in the back of our head that tells us to back off and not engage, or to compromise at best. Our lizard brain is totally irrational and often contradicts reality.

For example, consider how many times you have backed off of introducing a new idea at work in fear that it might be rejected, ignored, or laughed at by management. Some of us have even entertained the thought that our ideas might even get us fired! Is this really the case? How many people have you seen get fired or ridiculed for introducing an idea that might better the company? Irrational? Of course!

People who appease the lizard brain end up delaying new launches, embedding destructive fear or pessimism in the work culture, and filling time with unnecessary meetings that produce a mirage of production.

Godin rightly points out that our job is to quiet and ignore the lizard brain. Here's how I try to put the lizard brain to rest:

- **Articulate the issue.** I try to articulate in writing my creative resistance. I find that this is extremely helpful in identifying core issues and underlying presuppositions.

- **Seek feedback.** Once the issue is articulated, I take my thoughts to a handful of trusted individuals to gain feedback about my struggle. In most cases, they quickly identify my irrational thoughts and give me much needed critique and encouragement on what to do next.

- **Write it down.** After receiving feedback, I go back and write some more to document my conclusions. In some cases, I will literally print out my convictions and place them where they will remind me of what I need to do.

Now that you are sensing a little bit of hope, in the next chapter I want to step back and give you a closer look at the way I process my insecurities as an idea maker and quiet the lizard brain.

---

[2]Google "Lizard Brain," and you will see numerous articles and video talks by Seth on this concept.

Good Idea (key thoughts from this section)	Now What? (your ideas and next steps for execution)
When it comes to ideas, only the strong survive.	_____ _____ _____
Are the enemies of our ideas real or just imagined?	_____ _____ _____
People who appease the lizard brain end up delaying new launches, embedding destructive fear or pessimism in the work culture, and filling time with unnecessary meetings that produce a mirage of production.	_____ _____ _____

The Dreaded Look Inside

Yes, I admit it. I'm insecure.

I struggle every day with how others will react to my ideas.

For me, ideas are very personal. They carry some of my most intimate thoughts about the world and what I think could be done to make it better. Whether I'm meeting with a client or a close friend, sharing my ideas is, in essence, sharing a part of my soul.

I'm also mindful that ideas have consequences. Many ideas create a domino effect of subsequent actions that could literally change the course of history. Life-altering decisions are made because of new ideas. They challenge, form, and guide our lives. Ideas are powerful and need to be respected.

Writing this book was a jump into unfamiliar waters for me. Although I blog regularly, I never really considered myself an author. Quite honestly, I still don't. I can't tell you how many times during this process I've felt inadequate and insecure about my writing and communication abilities. When my publisher first approached me to work on this book project, I was completely floored. "Who, me?" I thought to myself. I have to admit that I chuckled quite a bit.

Even as I write this sentence, my mind is filled with questions about how well this book will be received and accepted. As I pushed past those uncomfortable feelings, I realized that working on this project has birthed several new insights about overcoming insecurity in the creative process.

If you're anything like me, the following thoughts will help you work through your insecurities and fears:

- **Insecurity is sometimes rooted in a false sense of pride.** It sounds paradoxical, but it's quite possible that our insecurity is rooted in an overexaggerated view of ourselves. We may be guilty of falsely projecting ourselves to be greater in influence than we actually are. Relax, more than 6 billion people in our world may never hear about your idea—nor even care to. As has been said, we would worry far less about what people think of us if we realized how seldom they do!

- **Insecurity may be a cover-up for our unwillingness to put in the hard work.** I have used insecurity as an excuse not to move on something. Many times, the issue had nothing to do with ability but was all about my willingness to engage.

- **Insecurity can be the result of not seeing the big picture.** As we will see later in this book, most great ideas need several people to jump on board in order to actualize the idea. The reality is that none of us have the whole idea. In fact, we are not able to follow through without the help of others and their respective skill sets. You don't have to know how to do everything.

- **Insecurity will not go away.** This is a good thing. I think all idea makers should be reminded regularly of their inadequacies. Leverage this understanding to think more collaboratively about your ideas. In addition, the need for help forces us to think more creatively. Some of the best solutions to our problems arise when we recognize the need. Therefore, insecurity that produces need is actually a great friend to the idea maker.

- **Moving forward despite the presence of insecurity, fears, and doubts will make us better human beings.** Almost all of the great idea makers I've been privileged to work with over the years have acknowledged this struggle with insecurity. Self-awareness in this area and understanding personal strengths and weaknesses have helped countless individuals move closer to actualizing their dreams.

The truth is that everyone is insecure at some level. People can cover it with all sorts of accolades and prestigious connections, but when we're alone, we all have to face this reality. Yes, everyone is still human.

But we can't let insecurity become the justification for not doing something with our ideas. Think about this: the alternative to *not* moving forward is living the life you never wanted. How horrific would that be?

The encouraging news is that those who choose to move forward with their ideas, despite insecurity, often gain confidence, clearer perspective, and timely relationships that fuel their efforts.

Good Idea (key thoughts from this section)	Now What? (your ideas and next steps for execution)
Ideas are very personal. They are also very powerful and need to be respected.	_____ _____ _____
All idea makers should be reminded regularly of their inadequacies—it will prompt them to think more collaboratively about their ideas.	_____ _____ _____
The alternative to *not* moving forward with your idea is living the life you never wanted. How horrific would that be?	_____ _____ _____

CHAPTER

13

Disturbance in the Force

G ood idea implementation requires a heavy investment of time, energy, and capital. Most idea makers quickly feel the gravitational pull toward a new life rhythm whenever they launch a new venture. One of the most noticeable areas in which this shift can be felt is in the idea maker's closest relationships.[1]

Whenever we start working on executing a new idea, it's inevitable that time and resources will be funneled to our new endeavor. As a result, it will often affect our ability to maintain the level of relationships we have around us. Whether they are taken away from the time formerly spent with one's family, friends, or colleagues, hours spent pursuing a new idea will naturally mean fewer hours with those who are used to a certain level of relational engagement.

This disturbance of the relational force (yes, I am a *Star Wars* geek!) can subconsciously cause those around you to communicate displeasure, friction, or even criticism toward your new idea. People who love you and want you to succeed may find themselves unknowingly pushing back at your efforts. It's not that they don't care; rather, they are processing what this new phase of life may mean for them and how they interact with you on a daily basis.

As an idea maker, if you simply recognize and acknowledge this dynamic, you'll probably be less prone to be disappointed and frustrated at those you love. I write this to remind you that ideas come at a cost,

---

[1]Stephen Pressfield has a very insightful section on this principle in his book *The War of Art*.

even relationally from time to time. Just be sure to remember that the resistance you sense may not really be a personal attack on your idea.

I first took notice of this relational disturbance a few years ago while leading an organization through a season of expansion into new areas. I began to notice that people who, in my opinion, should have been the most favorable to change weren't the ones most excited about it. Upon further conversations with key stakeholders, I began to realize that their hesitancy had very little to do with the idea of growth. In fact, most of them were in favor of where the organization was going. Their concern was with what it all meant for team dynamics and work culture. Some of them believed that they would have less access to key drivers of the organization and thus sensed a potential disconnect to the overall movement.

This new insight led me to spend more time clarifying vision and facilitating collaborative opportunities to build a deeper sense of ownership and access. Dave Blanchard, former business designer for IDEO, gave me some great advice during one of our conversations about this kind of relational tension. As he said, "In regards to people who are closest to you, overcommunication and total transparency are key." Relational tension is often the fruit of a lack of communication and a sense of abandonment.

Bringing It Home

The disturbance in the force can most definitely be felt at home as well. Most idea makers' spouses or significant others are far more calculated and less entrepreneurial in their choices than they will ever be. This means that they are regularly asking the idea makers how the ideas will be implemented and at what cost. They need—and deserve—to know what we're thinking and how we plan to get there (even if we don't have all the answers).

Early in my marriage, I just assumed my wife would magically know why and how I would pursue my ideas. (Insert laugh here.) She had to understand, right? After all, she was smart enough to choose me. (Insert hysterical laugh here.)

In actuality, her lack of understanding of my efforts had nothing to do with her intelligence. It had more to do with *my* lack of wisdom toward incorporating her into my process. Needless to say, I began to sense growing frustration from her, especially in seasons when I was consumed by a new project. Passing comments of frustration came out in the shape of pessimism about an idea or redirected conversations about home life (or lack thereof).

My initial response was defensive. I began to internally question why she wasn't supportive of my ideas. The last person I expected to be critical was my own wife. These were very discouraging moments. Fortunately, as I began to reassess the way I work, I soon realized that I had not communicated enough to the person closest to me. As obvious as it may have appeared, I had been guilty of doing the very thing I was advising others not to do.

My wife and I now communicate regularly about new ventures. Not only has this practice improved our marriage, but it has also allowed me to be more intentional in clarifying my intentions and processes to others. I regularly communicate to my wife about ideas, systems, and workload so that she is aware of when I may be more consumed outside the home. She also recognizes that these seasons come and go. She is committed to helping me navigate opportunities while guarding my bandwidth. I have asked my wife to be openly critical and probing in her engagement with my ideas. I know that the clearer she is in understanding my path, the better we can work toward things that ultimately benefit our family and relationship.

Good Idea (key thoughts from this section)	Now What? (your ideas and next steps for execution)
Whenever they launch a new venture, idea makers quickly feel the gravitational pull toward a new life rhythm—particularly as it concerns their closest relationships.	
People who love you and want you to succeed may find themselves unknowingly pushing back at your efforts.	
Relational tension is often the fruit of a lack of communication and a sense of abandonment. Overcommunication and transparency are the keys to fixing this.	

CHAPTER 14

Hear Me Out

N o one enjoys criticism.

No one is getting up in the morning thinking, "I hope I get heavily criticized today!"

Nonetheless, any meaningful idea worth developing will get criticized at some point. In a world where the customer is king, it's no wonder many feel a sense of entitlement to voice their critiques openly, even when those critiques are unjustified. Whether it's a standard, style, or service, it has become commonplace to feel that we have a right to criticize if our expectations are not met. It doesn't matter how familiar or unfamiliar we are with a product or idea; our experience tends to trump everything else.

I am not writing this to say that we should just brush off criticism. Rather, learning how to listen well to critiques, even from strangers, can become extremely beneficial as we work to improve our ideas. Later in the book, I will share some thoughts about how to deal with conflict and tension in a team setting. In the meantime, here are some practical ways to turn the tables on criticism to our benefit, especially in public engagement:

- **Discern the difference between a critique of your *idea* and a direct attack on *you* as an idea maker.** If it is the former, then you should welcome it with open arms. It's possible that your critic sees something that you may have missed. If this is the case, be sure to thank him or her openly and make the appropriate changes necessary to move the idea forward. If it is the latter, you will have to decide on the appropriate response. For example, if it appears that the critic is ill informed, a kind response of clarification will often take care of the misperception. On the other hand, if the critic is on the offensive, especially in a public platform like a blog or on social media, it's better to take the conversation offline. Be sure to publicly communicate your intent to provide clarification offline. If the attack is vicious in nature, it's probably best to ignore them. Most people will recognize the negative nature of the engagement and understand why you're choosing not to respond.

- **Think change before defense.** If the goal of any engagement is to better your idea or product, commentary should not discourage you. In fact, be sure to regularly invite constructive criticism about your work from your customer or supporter base. I like the approach Skype has taken recently for feedback. After each call, there's a quick, one-click survey that comes up asking about the quality of the call. There's very little need to respond defensively if the goal is to improve the product.

- **Always side on respect.** No one wins when you start acting like a jerk. In most cases, it will further hurt your brand. Stay gracious and acknowledge the fact that the person took time to provide input. Be sure to communicate your desire to improve your work and invite that person to help you do it.

The Other Side of the Coin (Practicing What We Preach)

Every so often, I find myself being unfairly critical about someone else's work. In retrospect, many of these moments of nonconstructive criticism were rooted in my insecurity and envy of the other person's success. The success of others is difficult to swallow for most competitive entrepreneurs. Our pride often convinces us that if we were given the same set of circumstances as the person we are envious of, we would have been as successful—if not more.

Have you ever been guilty of this?

Whether you've been on the side of being unfairly critical or on the side of sensing the envy of others, the reality is that these kinds of engagements quickly become infantile and unproductive (if not plain mean) for the parties involved.

I have to confess that there were moments earlier in my life when I intentionally played with and pressed into the envy I sensed from others to evoke a response. In other words, I rubbed it in! As a result, I caused more unnecessary strife and pain in these relationships. I told you this could get infantile.

Fortunately, I'm getting better as I get older. I find myself playing the comparison and envy game less and less often as the years go by. Here's why:

- It's not worth the energy. There are so many other things we could and should be consumed with that have far more noble purposes than criticizing others.
- Nonconstructive criticism is just that—nonconstructive.
- The issue is usually *my* issue and not theirs. Criticism reveals more about the criticizer's character than the person being criticized.
- Most of the conflict is fictional and imaginary. It is not rooted in reality. It's more perceptions than fact. No one knows the whole story.
- You can become a whole lot more productive and stronger if you celebrate the good of your competitor. Who knows? You might actually learn a thing or two.
- The envy of others can give you a false sense of success. Just because someone thinks you're successful doesn't mean you actually are.
- You're unlikely to change the other person anyway.

Life is far too short to be spent in such shallow forms of engagement. Focus on working on your ideas and let others deal with criticism. Decide to live in optimism and look on the bright side of anything that comes up in life. Put your energy toward productive good and seeing the good in others. I promise that life will be far more enjoyable this way.

Good Idea (key thoughts from this section)	Now What? (your ideas and next steps for execution)
Learning how to listen well to critiques, even from strangers, can become extremely beneficial as we work to improve our ideas.	

(continued)

(continued)

Good Idea (key thoughts from this section)	Now What? (your ideas and next steps for execution)
If the goal of a criticism is to better your idea or product, commentary should not discourage you.	_____ _____ _____
Focus on working on your ideas and let others do the criticizing.	_____ _____ _____

Taking It Further

Have you ever backed away from introducing a new idea at work in fear that it might be rejected, ignored, or laughed at by management? What might have motivated this?

Articulate in writing the creative resistance you are experiencing. Then send those thoughts to a few trusted friends for their feedback and help in identifying any irrational thoughts you might be experiencing.

Have you ever allowed insecurity to become the justification for not doing something with your ideas? Recall that idea now. If you had implemented it, how would your life—or the world—be different?

What relationships will pursuing your new idea jeopardize? How can you proactively address this tension before it gets bad?

Think of a recent criticism. How did you respond? What was the outcome?

Paving a Creative Pathway

No Escape Clause

"**I** don't have time to work on that."
"I'm just not that organized."
"I'm more of a visionary."
Sound familiar?

It all sounds so reasonable, doesn't it? Who can fault the idea lover for being real about his or her own makeup and circumstances? Aren't creatives exempt from having to be organized?

Nope.

It doesn't matter how well we master the art of the creative excuse. It won't get us any closer to actualizing our ideas. There's no way around it. You must organize your creative process. Period. Unfortunately, too many people have given themselves—in the name of creativity—a false sense of permission not to be organized. Organization doesn't have to be the arch nemesis of creativity. In fact, organization and creativity must work hand in hand for any idea to become reality.

There are no magical potions, incantations, or secrets that remove the necessity for some semblance of structure in the creative process. Think about any creative individuals or companies that you admire. Do they have some kind of creative process? I thought so.

Most memorable creatives throughout history had a system for implementing ideas. View systems as a means of disciplining your art and skill set. Developing these healthy habits will, in the long run, free you to be who you want to be. Just as discipline ultimately gives musicians the freedom to express their souls, systems provide the same kind of freedom for idea makers.

To paraphrase a quote from Edison, ideas are 1 percent inspiration and 99 percent perspiration. Perspiration is the fuel that allows inspiration to move forward.

So, how does one organize creativity? Here are some beginning principles to consider:

- **Confession is good for the heart and a great place to start.**

  "Hello, my name is Charles and I have a problem with organizing my creativity." The first step to recovery is admitting that you have a problem. Stop making excuses. The energy that it takes to rationalize could be used to implement ideas, even the impossible ones.

- **Find some help.**

  If organization is an area of weakness, take a couple of weeks to talk to people you consider to be highly organized and ask them how they do it. Ask them what tools and systems they find the most helpful. Being around idea makers who are more interested in implementing than chatting about theoretical ideas will inspire and challenge you. If you're serious about seeing your ideas come to life, you'll find that most will be more than willing to help you along the way. Don't be shy in asking.

  Focus on action. My friend Scott Belsky, author of the best-selling book, *Making Ideas Happen*,[1] regularly writes and speaks about our need to be biased toward action. He emphasizes the immense benefits of posturing one's life toward action. Although it may sound self-evident, having a bias toward action can really change the way we live. A bias toward action has allowed me to be far more proactive and productive in my own work.

  This has affected the way I approach meetings. First, I no longer call meetings that aren't necessary. (Yes, I've been guilty of calling meetings just because they were scheduled on the calendar.) If a meeting does not generate meaningful action that

---

[1]Scott Belsky, *Making Ideas Happen: Overcoming the Obstacles Between Vision and Reality.* New York: Penguin Group, 2010.

furthers the mission of a company or organization, it has no business existing in the first place.

Second, I moved from having one person taking notes for everyone else on the team to everyone at the meeting taking notes. Productivity requires one to be able to identify and create tangible next steps for contextualized follow-through. This can't be the work of one person. Each leader must take initiative to actively listen and write down his or her own action steps. This shift has greatly increased both the level of engagement and productivity. (Plus, who really reads the memo with notes sent after a meeting? Exactly!)

Third, each meeting produces a collaborative list of things that must get done to move an idea forward. Seeing visible action on a whiteboard (or at least on paper) can hold the group accountable to next steps.

As the title of this book suggests, any good idea maker must continue to ask, "Now what?" Action is essential.

- **Accept the reality of refinement.**

There is no perfect way to be organized. We have to accept the fact that refining our organizational skills will be a lifelong endeavor. We'll never get there. An imperfect system that seeks improvement is far better than not having a system at all.

Although these are not magical steps for idea making, I hope you do something today to move your ideas forward. As you move forward, a system will rise to the surface that will help you organize your creativity and implement your ideas.

Always remember that your idea is too important not to surround it with organization.

Good Idea (key thoughts from this section)	Now What? (your ideas and next steps for execution)
Organization and creativity must work hand in hand for any idea to become reality.	_____
	_____
	_____

(continued)

(continued)

Good Idea (key thoughts from this section)	Now What? (your ideas and next steps for execution)
Just as discipline ultimately gives musicians the freedom to express their souls, systems provide the same kind of freedom for idea makers.	_____ _____ _____
Perspiration is the fuel that allows inspiration to move forward.	_____ _____ _____

Got Rhythm?

A ll of us have rhythm.

Let me clarify. All of us have life rhythm.

I believe that for each of us there are specific times and environ-ments that are optimal—times in which we thrive in our work. These are the various segments of our day where energy and mental focus are at their highest. It's when we get our best work done. Being aware and taking advantage of these opportune moments can exponentially increase productivity and speed of delivery.

For example, I am at my most creative in the morning. Once lunch hits, I tend to slow down greatly. It's not that I can't be productive in the afternoon; it just takes noticeably more effort for me to get things done later in the day. This is why I try to do my most creative work in the morning. I generally try to use the afternoon to catch up on things that don't demand as much creative energy, such as responding to e-mails, scheduling appointments, conducting project update meetings, and doing basic bookkeeping. I also like meeting people in the afternoon because I don't have to carry the energy alone.

I usually find my second wind late in the evening after my family goes to bed. I often use this time to engage any new ideas or catch up on project development. I set a time limit for late-night work to ensure that I do get some rest for the next day.

I've also identified the environments where I work best. I tend to go to the same locations, whether it's a coffee shop or meeting space, because I've learned that I have less trouble settling in to work. I suppose it's similar to muscle memory. Working in similar environments minimizes the time necessary to get focused.

I also enjoy working on airplanes. Knowing that I can't just get up and leave (that would be bad) forces me to focus on completing work. I actually like the jet engine noise because it tends to drown out further distractions. Although I don't particularly like to travel, time to work on a plane is definitely a benefit. As you might guess, several chapters in this book were written during flights.

The takeaway point here is that we all need to learn what works best for us. Once we figure out some of that, we then have to commit to leveraging it for productive behavior. *Knowing* the best times and environments is worlds apart from actually *restructuring* one's schedule. This is true for us as individuals as well as teams.

In working with teams, I've found it important to figure out how my peers work as it relates to their own personal rhythms. This is why I tend to shy away from mundane meetings in the morning (actually, most meetings period). If our team meets in the morning, I want it to be about creative dreaming and projection of potential concepts. Of course, this doesn't always work if you have creatives who don't function well in the morning. Fortunately for me, I can work morning or late night. At a minimum, you really want to find out which portions of the day your team wants to avoid for creative meetings. I suspect that it might be midafternoon for most.

Regardless, teams need to talk this through and see when they are most creative, productive, and engaged. For some, any conversation about ideas can be invigorating, regardless of time. Even if this is true for you, it might not be true for your entire team.

Although there will be times when we don't have a choice for optimal times of engagement, it is important to be self-aware enough to strategically plan one's day when possible. If you work for someone else and have a voice in the process, why not nudge your boss to consider this?

Years ago, when I used to just go with the flow and not pay attention to life rhythm, this is how my day looked:

6:30 AM—Get up and get kids ready for school.

8:30 AM—Arrive at office, open laptop, and start answering e-mails.

9:30 AM—Start focusing on work for the day.

9:50 AM—Feel some momentum and productivity.

10:00 AM—Interrupt productivity to attend meetings.

12:00 PM—Lunch.

1:00 PM—Back at work trying to get stuff done while being distracted by social media.

2:00 PM—Still trying to focus.

3:00 PM—Finally focused but craving a coffee break.

3:30 PM—Catch up on e-mails.

4:30 PM—Make final push of work before going home.

5:30 PM—Leave work feeling way behind.

6:30 PM—Get home and have dinner with family.

7:30 PM—Try to catch up on work via phone between moments with family.

9:00 PM—Get kids ready for bed.

10:00 PM—Spend time with wife.

11:00 PM—Get back to catching up on work.

1:00 AM—Watch some ESPN.

2:00 AM—Finally get to bed for a few hours.

6:30 AM—Wake up exhausted to start the day again.

Sound familiar?

It's no wonder that people have to work around the clock. The issue isn't really about a lack of time, but a lack of focus and awareness. Add some unexpected life happenings to all of this and you'll end up in a world of hurt.

It will ultimately cost you something to live this way. What are you willing to give up? Your health? Your sanity? Your relationship with the very ones you're working so hard for?

Sobering.

Take a moment to write down *your* optimal times throughout the day, as well as your optimal environments for creative production. Afterward, open up your calendar to see if it matches up with your life rhythm. Do this with your team as well and see if you can collectively reach some conclusions that may help your company or organization become more productive. An awareness of your individual and corporate rhythm will keep things in perspective for everyone involved.

Last time I checked, none of us are superhuman. Don't forget that.

Good Idea (key thoughts from this section)	Now What? (your ideas and next steps for execution)
Being aware and taking advantage of the opportune moments during the day when you thrive in your work can exponentially increase productivity and speed of delivery.	
Working in the same or a similar environment minimizes the time necessary to get focused.	
Knowing the best times and environments for you is worlds apart from actually *restructuring* your schedule.	

CHAPTER 17

Don't Just Add; Multiply

"**D**o you think you could do me a big favor?"
"Of course, whatever you want."

"Would you be interested in helping me start this project?"
"No problem, I'll make time. What is it?"

"I have an idea. I know it's extra work, but I think it has great potential."
"I'd love to be a part of whatever you're doing! I'm sure I can shuffle some things around and make it work. So, what's your idea?"

"What do you do for a living?"
"Well, I am a _____, _____, and _____, and I also _____, _____, and _____."

Whenever I hear these kinds of questions and statements, red flags go up in my mind.

A Wandering Generality

I once heard an interview with Seth Godin in which he paraphrased Zig Ziglar, saying: "Don't be a wandering generality. Rather, be a meaningful specific." His point? It's better to do a few things really well rather than do many things with mediocrity.

Being remarkable at something requires focus and commitment over the long haul. It's highly unlikely that a person will achieve this without giving something up. In fact, it will probably require the sacrifice of many things.

Surface-level adoption of many ideas only adds more hours of work. Focused commitment to a couple of ideas multiplies productivity.

Let's be honest. This is the quandary of many idea lovers.

Idea lovers just can't get enough of it. It's totally addictive and hard to resist.

Yes, I'm talking about new ideas (a.k.a. flashes of genius—at least, that's what it feels like at the moment). For people enthralled by ideas, the flickering appearance of more ideas is far too often irresistible. What could be so wrong with adding new concepts to a project or adding another whole new project? We need more ideas, don't we?

Well . . . yes and no.

It's true that new ideas can greatly benefit an endeavor. In fact, new ideas—especially those that strategically refine or add value to a project—are necessary. Unfortunately, many of these idea flashes can also be very distracting and energy-draining, and some can even derail a project from its original goal. Most idea flashes feel great because they inject adrenaline into the minds and hearts of those experiencing them.

The Bad News . . .

Like any other high, there's usually a let down. So, what do addicts do after a let down? They go back for more.

For idea lovers, this means more meetings and more ideas. Eventually, team members will either feel overwhelmed by the amount of work or start to characterize meetings as solely hype since most of the ideas won't get implemented anyway. A continuation along the path toward idea flashes will end in discouragement, tension, and disconnectedness by everyone involved. When it comes to a new idea, you can cry wolf only so many times.

Advice?

Here are a couple of things you (and your team) can do to stay focused and multiply impact rather than simply add more hours to the workload:

- **Don't forget the objective(s).** Objectives are important. In fact, they're vital to the success of any idea. Objectives are the goals of one's mission. Objectives (or goals) provide much-needed guidance, healthy boundaries, and measurable outcomes (both quantitatively and qualitatively). Working on an idea without an objective is like taking a shot in the dark. Here are some questions to consider:

o How does the idea support the objectives of the endeavor?

o Are there elements of the idea that could actually hurt the mission?

o Are the objectives measurable?

o Do the objectives provide healthy boundaries for engaging the idea's breadth or scope?

o Why are we working on this idea again?

o How will our ideas be accountable to the objectives?

o Are there any guiding questions or processes developed in this area of aligning ideas with objectives and objectives to mission?

• **Stay neutral and press pause.** When you experience one of these idea flashes, record it and revisit it later. If it's good, it'll stick around. In other words, let it brew a little in your mind before diving fully into it. Refuse the urge to say yes or no on the spot, especially during meetings. Believe me, your team will thank you for this. All of us need some time, especially with significant ideas, to process and decide accordingly. Develop a simple system that allows you to document and filter new concepts. Here are some suggestions:

o Take the 3 minutes it takes to write down (or type) your idea. I usually carry around a Moleskine brand notebook with a specific section dedicated to new ideas. I also try to record the idea on my laptop. I use a simple note-taking program to keep things organized. Several programs allow you to tag ideas with appropriate categories so that you can easily find them later. Quite honestly, you could probably use one document as a temporary holding place until you have time to categorize your ideas later.

o Regularly review your ideas. I have a scheduled time every week to revisit new ideas and opportunities. I will often schedule these during my travel times because I find that I am more focused while on the road. I usually use the time at the airport waiting to board or the time on the flight itself to review recent ideas. I try not to spend more than 30 minutes on this. If an idea begins to stir my heart, I will then set aside time later that week to work on it more with purpose.

o During meetings, I take the advice of Scott Belsky, who suggests that teams write down new ideas and place them in a back burner column in the notes.[1] This way, teams can stay focused on the project at hand without becoming too distracted. Teams can meet later to specifically explore these new ideas.

- **Think integration and not adoption.** A new idea doesn't have to be a whole new add-on to your current work. Think of ways to integrate elements of the new concepts into your work instead of figuring out ways to adopt the whole enchilada. I've found that this helps keep me focused on the overall objectives while keeping projects moving forward. If the new idea is from another party, be sure to clarify expectations and deliverables. The upcoming section on collaboration will further explain how this might work.

Discovering the Power of Focus

Pursuing a dream is never easy.

Any significant endeavor requires a deep gut check and exploration into one's passions and motives for living life. I've made some tough decisions in cutting away elements and opportunities that I deeply cared about in order to pursue my dreams.

During a recent season of change, I came to rediscover the power of focus, especially as it relates to multiplying productivity. My assumption had been that reallocating the number of hours from my numerous areas of work and funneling them to my new focus would simply add that many hours of value to my new endeavor. In other words, I thought adding 20 more hours to my passion would produce something equivalent of 20 more hours of work. Fortunately, I was mistaken.

In actuality, 20 more hours of focused work exponentially produces much more than a scattered collection of hours. I'm finding that focusing on one thing over a longer period multiplies productivity and quality.

---

[1]Scott Belsky offers several helpful insights like this in his book, *Making Ideas Happen: Overcoming the Obstacles Between Vision and Reality* (New York: Penguin, 2010).

Yes, I completely understand that this sounds like a luxury for most entrepreneurs. I know that getting to this place of full-time launching takes a long time and requires a deep level of sacrifice. It took me more than 18 months of fiscal belt tightening, sleepless nights, and sacrificial investments to have the ability to start something I completely believe in. I have fully felt the tension between wanting to dive into something that makes one's heart beat faster and the reality of sustaining one's life, especially those of us with families. I acknowledge that this is an incredibly difficult decision for most.

Nevertheless, if you can do your homework and position your life to be able to do it, going full bore for a season is not a bad idea. Personally, I think it's worth the risk to pursue a passion for a year or two. Figure out what you really need—minimally—to survive and budget your life so that you can take a greater step into your dreams. It may take you a year or two to get to that place, but I'm convinced it's worth it. You will feel more alive and productive than you ever have if you choose to focus on something for a season and even allow other good things to wait.

I know many of you can juggle a hundred things. Just because you can doesn't mean you should. Plus, let's be honest, becoming the best at something can't be accomplished when you're juggling multiple interests.

Let's continue to posture our lives toward focusing more and becoming distracted less.

Good Idea (key thoughts from this section)	Now What? (your ideas and next steps for execution)
Being remarkable at something requires focus and commitment over the long haul.	
Surface-level adoption of many ideas only adds more hours of work. Focused commitment to a couple of ideas multiplies productivity.	

(continued)

(continued)

Good Idea (key thoughts from this section)	Now What? (your ideas and next steps for execution)
When you experience an idea flash, record it and revisit it later. If it's good, it'll stick around and be there later when you have time to process it.	_____ _____ _____
Figure our what you really need— minimally—to survive and budget your life so that you can take a greater step into your dreams.	_____ _____ _____

CHAPTER
18

I Can See It!

"A picture is worth a thousand words."

This well-known adage highlights the power of visuals to communicate complex ideas and large amounts of data quickly to the observer. Visuals provide perspective, invite engagement, and possess the power to move the viewer toward action. Whether through words, images, or symbols, visuals have the power to clarify concepts and ignite direction.

Most of the idea makers whom I've had the privilege of working with have visuals that continue to inspire their creative endeavors as well as keep them focused. The following is a list of some of the visual helps I've seen over the years:

- A wall dedicated to visually outlining a creative process with colored Post-it notes of a current project that highlight progress
- An object that points back to a moment that inspired the birth of a company
- Nicely framed pictures on the office wall of people being benefited by an organization's work, with a brief synopsis that includes their names and stories
- Memorable quotes displayed throughout the building that highlight the ethos of a company
- Intentional architectural design that allows employees to more naturally develop a work culture that embodies a company's values

- Calendars printed on large sheets of paper or drawn out on whiteboard IdeaPaint–treated walls that display and welcome team member feedback and interaction
- Whiteboard or glass space for team members to note and refine new ideas
- Iconic and/or coded symbols throughout a workspace that point to a current project or campaign

I personally like to tape up visuals from current projects or items that have recently inspired me to think differently. It may be an image, quote, or even an article that has challenged my thinking. If it's important enough, I will even take it along with me as I drive or travel. I'm visually driven, so having physical reminders around me has become extremely helpful in keeping me on track. Another benefit is that these visuals tend to be great conversation starters with people who see them. More often than not, others will add more insight and value to what I deem important.

More Than Digital

Digital is great, but there's something about holding a physical object that brings it home for me. Educators have told us for years that adding more senses to an experience makes it more memorable. Why not add this to your creative process?

Right now, some of you are thinking, *How will I find time to do this?*

The good news is that visuals will probably save you time in the long run because they will keep you more focused and growing. Once you develop this habit, it usually ends up feeling effortless. It becomes a part of your daily rhythm.

To actualize, first visualize.

Good Idea (key thoughts from this section)	Now What? (your ideas and next steps for execution)
Visuals provide perspective, invite engagement, and possess the power to move the viewer toward action.	_____ _____ _____

Good Idea (key thoughts from this section)	Now What? (your ideas and next steps for execution)
Visuals have the power to clarify concepts and ignite direction.	_____ _____ _____
To actualize, first visualize.	_____ _____ _____

chapter 19

Press Pause

"Wax on. Wax off. Breathe in. Breathe out."

Do you remember Pat Morita's role as Mr. Miyagi in the original *Karate Kid*? Classic.

He took a teen named Daniel LaRusso (played by Ralph Macchio), who was being harassed by neighborhood bullies who knew karate, and trained him to win the very karate championship all those teens were in at the end of the movie. I hope I'm not spoiling this for you. Then again, the original movie is nearly 30 years old.

During the first several days of Daniel's training, Mr. Miyagi had him wax all his cars while focusing in on his breathing. Of course, in classic Hollywood fashion, despite Daniel's frustration with these odd exercises, everything comes full circle to sweet victory. Daniel realizes that some of his martial arts moves were rooted in the same arm movement of waxing. In addition, the ability to breathe calmly in pressure situations comes back to help him win the final fight.

The point?

Something as elementary as breathing allowed Daniel to accomplish a major goal in his life, even in the midst of great pressure and pain. I think we all remember his one-legged crane kick at the end of the movie. The very thing that appeared to be a complete waste of time and energy became the foundation upon which a dream became reality.

Sometimes actions that feel counterintuitive or counterproductive are necessary. As paradoxical as it sounds, ideas need space. They need space and time to breathe, refine, and grow. A full-court press on your ideas could suffocate and limit its innovation. Create some space. Step away and breathe again. Your idea needs it.

Too much time spent on an idea without a break often leads to frustration, tension, and unnecessary anxiety. Ideas take time to develop and need space through the process. It's okay to say, "Let's revisit this idea tomorrow."

Take a time-out. Pause. Stop. (Or whatever you want to call it.)

Here are some ways that you can incorporate space for your ideas.

- **Plan ahead when possible.** Outside of last-minute edits, do your best to create a process that will allow you to plan ahead. If you're a creative, is there a process that allows you to develop concepts without making things up at the last minute? Do you have a timeline of incremental milestones and not just deadlines?

- **Invite outside voices.** Although there may be some areas of confidentiality, are you able to invite outside voices, even voices outside your field, to discuss elements of your idea? I often invite or hire outside consultants to help me better think about my concepts. That kind of investment usually goes a long way toward idea implementation. If your budget is low, I hope you have enough relational capital to draw from to help you out. In addition, take some regular time to read outside of your field. I subscribe to a handful of blogs in areas I don't professionally work in. These unrelated fields help me to create space in my thinking about the projects I'm involved in.

- **Walk away.** If time allows, walk away from your idea development. Work on something completely different for a couple of days. Give your idea and yourself some space to reconsider. If you're a serial entrepreneur, I dare you to take a weekend off!

Your Life Needs Space as Well

Life in our world today is undoubtedly pressing and overwhelming. The increasing number of tasks, responsibilities, and expectations put on individuals by our culture (and ourselves) can often crush our ability to enjoy life—the very thing many of us are working so hard to accomplish. Ironic.

The truth of the matter is that no one will ever have enough time to do everything his or her heart desires. Period. Yes, we need to get over the omni-mentality that many of us carry. Trying to do everything for an idea while saying yes to everyone else and their ideas will eventually kill you (maybe even literally).

All of us need moments to just pause. I'm not necessarily referring to vacations here, but simply moments to breathe and reflect. Quite honestly, many of us even vacation hard, leaving very little flexibility in our plans to actually enjoy time away. Often, it's more about task accomplishment on vacation than relaxation. There's actually no vacating of any kind for some of us!

Emergency Room Counseling

I'll be honest (not that I was lying before). It's difficult for me to practice spatial ideation—giving my ideas some time and space to breathe. I want to be in the grind. I want to work on ideas nonstop. I love what I do. My ego tells me that I can work through obstacles such as mental blocks and fatigue. Once in motion, I never want to stop. The Energizer bunny has nothing on me. At least, that's what I used to think.

A few years ago, I found myself working three jobs that added up to approximately 80 hours a week. I felt fine. I didn't feel stressed, so I kept on going. One day I started to feel a tingling sensation on both of my hands. I didn't think too much of it, but eventually, I experienced paralysis on both hands. Upon my wife's gentle nudge (actually, it was more like a command!), I admitted myself into the emergency room.

The doctors did all kinds of tests and put me on IV. They came back and told me the paralysis was caused by stress.

"What?! How could that be since I don't feel stressed?" I asked.

One of my doctors during a follow-up visit sat me down and explained. He started by calling me a freak of nature. My doctor said that my mind had been trained to override anything my body was communicating to it. I didn't feel stressed because my mind had refused to listen to my body. He said that unless I drastically changed the way I live, I would end up in a world of hurt. Hint, hint.

My life changed that day. I began to intentionally alter my day-to-day activities. I cut away one of my jobs and took focused time away. I started taking several moments throughout each day to slow down my body. I tried to listen to my body even though I couldn't hear it speaking to me. I took time to even think about my breathing. Yes, breathe in and breathe out. It may sound silly, but pausing saved my life.

I'm concerned that many of you reading this book are headed toward the emergency room. In fact, it wouldn't surprise me if many of you have already been there. We need to pause regularly, both for ourselves and for our ideas.

Putting on the Breaks!

Here are some practical ways to pause more in your life:

- Shut the office door, turn off the lights, and close your eyes for 5 minutes. I know what you're thinking. You'll fall asleep because you're so tired. If you're that tired, you really need to rearrange your life. Let's compromise. Keep your eyes open.

- Go to the car for a few minutes and just sit. Open the windows and just be still.

- Stop by a park for 10 minutes during lunch when someone cancels an appointment. Don't fill your calendar with another appointment. It's okay. The world will function without another meeting.

- Put on a headset and listen to a favorite song, preferably a song that reminds you of why you do what you do.

- Take a 5- to 10-minute walk around your workplace. Smile a little. It's going to be okay.

Simple paused moments will make a world of difference for you and your idea. Destiny is found in the collective result of the small, intentional decisions you make in life.

Good Idea (key thoughts from this section)	Now What? (your ideas and next steps for execution)
Ideas need space and time to breathe, refine, and grow. A full-court press on your ideas could suffocate and limit their innovation.	

Good Idea (key thoughts from this section)	Now What? (your ideas and next steps for execution)
The increasing number of tasks, responsibilities, and expectations put on individuals by our culture (and ourselves) can often crush our ability to enjoy life—the very thing many of us are working so hard to accomplish.	_____ _____ _____
Trying to do everything for an idea while saying yes to everyone else and their ideas will eventually kill you.	_____ _____ _____

Taking It Further

Write down all the excuses you have used to give yourself permission to be disorganized. (See Chapter 15 for a list to remind you.) Take that list and shred it. Now you have no excuses.

Find a creative who is producing consistently and ask that person what system or process he or she uses to get things done. Try it.

Take a moment to write down your optimal times throughout the day, as well as your optimal environments for creative production. Afterward, open your calendar to see if it matches up with your life rhythm. Do this with your team as well and see if you can collectively reach some conclusions that may help your company or organization become more productive.

Look at your list of projects. Which ones stir your heart? Which do you wish you had never agreed to?

Think of a visual that symbolizes or expresses your idea. How can you integrate that visual into your workflow or promotional efforts?

Simple moments of pausing will make a world of difference for you and your idea. Try one of the ideas at the end of Chapter 19 today and make it a habit in your life.

Elements for Idea Making 1

CHAPTER 20

The Art of Evolution

I love entrepreneurs.

Entrepreneurs are by far some of the most passionate people you'll ever meet. I love being around like-minded people who aren't afraid to venture into new, uncharted areas. Their boldness, tenacity, and creativity often stir deep inspiration and much-needed challenge for my life.

Unfortunately, not everyone who calls himself or herself an entrepreneur is one. Many are really idea lovers who are stuck, for one reason or another, in their pursuit. The lizard brain is on full alert in their lives! For many, the overwhelming fear of not knowing the full extent of what they're getting into has become paralyzing.

Here's a little secret about entrepreneurship (and idea making): it's impossible to fully know what to expect until you're already in implementation mode. In other words, no amount of prep work will clear all of the questions you have about your venture. In fact, it's possible that over-analysis of an idea may create an inability to move forward. Paradoxically, it's in the very act of implementation that makes it possible to frame the right questions you'll need for your journey. Here are some reasons why:

- **The idea you start with will rarely be the same idea you end up with.** All ideas evolve, and this evolution will require new questions and perspectives to adapt with it as the idea grows. Don't stress about having all the answers before you begin. In fact, you probably don't even have all of the *questions* you need to make your idea a reality! These will come to light as you start to implement.

87

- **Many questions prior to implementation are hypothetical at best.** People spend a lot of time considering scenarios that may never take place. In fact, many of them *will* never take place. Although it's good to have a general sense of what may occur, you don't have to be the world's top expert on your idea before you start. Give yourself some slack. It's okay not to be completely sure; move forward anyway. This may feel counterintuitive, but it will make more sense as you feel momentum. Keep moving and planning at the same time.

- **There's plenty of help along the way.** Unless you're thinking of embarking on something absolutely unique to this world, you don't have to carry out a plan alone. Plan on bringing in timely voices to help you as new problems and opportunities arise. Take time to breathe and reflect on your process. Celebrate the lessons you learned along the way and record those insights.

Ideas are organic. They will continue to adapt to their environments. The idea that *was* is not the idea that *is*, nor is it the idea it will *eventually be*.

I'm not saying that you shouldn't do your homework before launching a new venture. In fact, you should have a clear overall sense of what you're pursuing and what you're bringing to the table. But too many potential idea makers unnecessarily get stuck because they feel the need to control the whole process. It's impossible to know the entire process, so get started. Move. Allow the right kinds of specific questions to arise along the way.

Good Idea (key thoughts from this section)	Now What? (your ideas and next steps for execution)
It's impossible to fully know what to expect until you're already in implementation mode.	_____
	_____
	_____
Unless you're thinking of embarking on something absolutely unique to this world, you don't have to carry out a plan alone.	_____
	_____
	_____

CHAPTER

21

DNA or R&D?

A re idea makers born or bred?

Tough question. Although it is true that some people appear to have an innate ability to carry out an idea, most appear to have intentionally developed a set of skills, perspectives, and values to drive their idea making.

It doesn't matter whether you're starting a company, organization, or campaign. Any idea-making endeavor appears to rise and fall on some common qualities in the person(s) driving the vision. While working up close with thousands of idea makers over the years, I've been able to identify some qualities among those who appear to be consistently successful implementers of concepts.

The following is an abbreviated list of some of these qualities:

- **Intuition Over Market Research.** This is not to say that successful idea makers don't do market research as they enter a new space. Rather, when push comes to shove, successful idea makers often side with their intuition even when the market tells them otherwise. They would rather make a countercurrent decision if it means that they could live without the regret of not having tried. Intuition for many may just be a fleeting notion, but to most idea makers, it is their guiding light.

- **Confidence to Adapt.** Most idea makers will be the first to admit that they don't have a complete strategy laid out in a business school kind of way. What they do have is a clear vision written down and a great sense of direction. Nevertheless, they have confidence in themselves to adapt and solve any problems that may come their way. They have a high sense of trust in their own abilities and recognize that they can go get help in areas where they lack knowledge or experience.

- **Undeniable Work Ethic.** Idea makers are some of the hardest working people I know. Most whom I've worked with have an achiever quality as one of their main strengths. An achiever is someone who tirelessly works to accomplish a goal and doesn't allow momentary obstacles and distractions to get in the way of actualizing an idea. Yes, idea makers are generally workaholics and don't mind sacrificing momentary pleasure for something greater. In addition, they are not driven purely by financial gain. Financial success may be the by-product of their pursuits but rarely the goal. The joy of making a meaningful idea come to life far outweighs any temporary benefits.

- **Commitment to Learning.** Idea makers are like giant sponges. They want to learn from everyone about almost anything. They recognize that they don't have all the answers and are willing to put themselves in the posture of a learner. This is why most successful idea makers are well read and regularly pursue more knowledge in their respective fields. They embody Harry Truman's saying: "Not all readers are leaders, but all leaders are readers." Idea makers thrive in this digital age where access to information is at an all-time high.

- **Collaboration as Need.** Most idea makers don't think collaboration is just a nice option. They know and openly admit that they need help from a strong network of people who are far more qualified than themselves. They have framed their lives to welcome the input and partnership of others.

- **Eternal Optimism.** Most idea makers see the cup as being half full and expect more water to pour in. They will not allow the negative focus of pessimists to get in the way of their efforts. Negativity, especially when nonconstructive, is not tolerated. Too much is at stake to exert energy toward criticism.

- **Tired But Happy.** Nothing can replace the joy of pursuing one's passion or dream. Although idea makers are often physically tired, they still have a spring in their step because they are fully alive. Idea makers remind us of what it means to live for what we believe in.

Do any of these qualities sound familiar to you? Is there an eerie sense that I might be describing you? You're probably reading this book because you are an idea maker. So let's keep moving!

Good Idea (key thoughts from this section)	Now What? (your ideas and next steps for execution)
When push comes to shove, successful idea makers often side with their intuition even when the market tells them otherwise.	_____ _____ _____
Most idea makers will be the first to admit that they don't have a complete strategy laid out in a business school kind of way. They do have a plan, but they recognize that adaptation is a part of the game.	_____ _____ _____
Nothing can replace the joy of pursuing one's passion or dream.	_____ _____ _____

CHAPTER

22

Risk (Overrated!)

"**Y**ou have to risk it all!"
    "Go all in!"
    "Take a leap of faith!"
"You're an entrepreneur. Don't go in halfway!"

The idea maker is often portrayed as an individual who risks everything. Is this really true?

Yes and no.

Although it is true that ideas require some level of risk taking, it's often not as risky as it appears from a distance. Most of the successful idea makers I've come across have learned to manage risk well. They have developed pathways to evaluate and minimize risk. In other words, it's possible that idea makers aren't necessarily greater risk takers than others. I think that many idea makers simply have a greater confidence in their own abilities to pursue an idea and a greater willingness to do the hard work of managing risk. Perhaps that self-confidence can be overblown at times, but it's really the work of managing risk that is the key. It begins with gathering information.

Show me the data!

Google has built an entire industry centered on the organization and aggregation of data. Numerous articles have highlighted Google's strength in analytics and how it ultimately guides the company decisions. Things at Google rarely happen on an artistic whim. The army of engineers and business gurus who guide the company rely heavily on data to minimize risk and maximize returns. It's not by accident that a particular number of sponsored search results show up each time you Google something. Every decision is backed by data.

Although there's no guarantee that everything coming out of Google will become a huge hit (Google Buzz is a good example), there's a good probability that most of the products and services will be met with wide acceptance.

Data don't guarantee the outcome of an idea, but they definitely provide great perspectives into possible and probable scenarios. Knowing this will give the idea maker incredible advantage over their competition.

Consider a company like Walmart that provides its vendors with nearly real-time data on product inventory and sales in all of their stores. For Walmart's vendors to gain reciprocal benefit and take full advantage of these data, they in turn must develop an infrastructure for effective point-of-sale (POS) analysis, predetermined key performance indicators, a strategy for sell-through issues, and of course, large amounts of space to store information. No, a spreadsheet will not do.

This kind of robust data gathering, mining, and distribution provides ample support for decision making. It's no wonder that Walmart's profits and influence continue to grow.

Your idea will need data that can help you make sound decisions. Don't just side with risk because it makes you feel more alive. Risk is cool until it kicks you in the gut. Uncalculated risk can become hazardous to your health.

I'm not saying that you can't be lucky and win the lottery with your idea. I'm also not saying that you need to have everything figured out at the onset. I'm simply saying that data can become a great ally toward making your ideas come to life. Why take risks when you don't have to?

Following are some ways to manage risk in the early stages of a start-up:

- **Do your homework.** There's no excuse for not learning as much as you can about your area of passion. In fact, you should seek to become an authority in that field. Why not? If you're committed to soaking in best practices and insights while sharing your findings with people who care, who says you can't become an authority in our digital age? (More on this in Part 8 of this book.)

  One of the main benefits of knowing your trade well is that it will significantly lower risk. The ability to see the current state of one's industry while being able to project where the field is going is a must for idea makers. If you are passionate about your work, supplement it with regular learning and networking with others in the field. Gather and analyze data and look for opportunities to integrate it into your decision making.

- **Know how to manage the money.** Yes, money. Even if finance is not your strength, you still have to continue to learn more about it. Period. Learning some basic skills in managing money, reading financial spreadsheets, forecasting budgets, and so on, will save the life of your company or organization. Seek immediate help if you don't feel proficient in this area.

- **Don't give up your day job (yet).** Many idea makers wait until the last minute to jump fully on board with a new venture. In other words, they don't just dive into a new opportunity simply because it's new. They recognize that ideas take time to develop and may require months, if not up to a year or two, before they are actually implemented. They choose to put in double time in order to position themselves to completely move over to their passion. The key here is to put in extra hours and not simply wait for the right time. In addition, there's usually a whole lot of cutting away financial excess during this time in order to save for the season of transition. As romantic as it may sound to drop everything to pursue a dream, most idea makers who have done well also planned well. I definitely don't want you to wait forever. I think wisdom lies somewhere between reckless risk and seeking perfection before launch.

- **Self-awareness is key.** Idea makers are self-aware enough to know what they do really well and what they don't. In areas that are not strengths, idea makers quickly look for people who can contribute expertise. It's important to add here that this does not mean that idea makers don't go out of their way to learn more about areas in which they are less informed. In fact, successful idea makers have a track record of learning enough about things they entrust to others to provide better direction and engage in more intelligent conversation. Gathering a great team greatly reduces risk for a venture.

- **Every penny counts, so keep pinching.** Unless they are independently wealthy or have money to blow, most idea makers do their best to lower overhead in running a business. I've heard (and personally lived out) stories of entrepreneurs doing everything from recycling paper clips they receive from others to bartering services with freelancers and vendors to collecting coupons. The point is that working toward increasing the bottom line is vital to the survival of a start-up. This is not to say that you shouldn't spend any money, but rather that it's important to minimize costs when possible. Costs for implementing an idea do add up quickly. Be mindful of how you spend your money.

Removing or minimizing unnecessary risk is just plain smart. It takes a lot of self-control to steward limited resources well. It all comes down to how badly you want to implement your passions.

Good Idea (key thoughts from this section)	Now What? (Your ideas and next steps for execution)
Idea makers aren't necessarily greater risk takers than others; they simply have a greater confidence in their own abilities to pursue an idea and a greater willingness to do the hard work of managing risk.	
Data don't guarantee the outcome of an idea, but they definitely give the idea maker an incredible advantage over the competition.	
There's no excuse to not learn as much as you can about your area of passion. In fact, you should seek to become an authority in that field. It is more possible than ever in our digital age.	

CHAPTER

23

The Miracle of Writing and Waiting

"I have a great idea. I was thinking the other day . . ."

"Great! Do you have anything written down that I could take a look at? I'd love to explore it a little further."

"Umm . . . I'm still working on it."

"No problem. Can you e-mail it to me when you get a chance?"

"Sure. I can send you something."

Months later . . . still waiting.

Sound familiar?

Many idea lovers are too quick to share their ideas. Although sharing an idea is essential to the idea-making process, being mindful of *when* and *how* to share is just as important. People who have a tendency to share their ideas immediately, without any sense of process, are probably less likely to actually implement the idea. Sharing ideas without processing them can trick our minds into thinking that we are actually doing something about an idea when in fact we are not.

Now, there are people who make the case that we should openly and quickly share our ideas with the public. Most of these individuals that I've seen (no naming names here) are either more developed in their thoughts than they appear or have broad influence that allows them to quickly implement after public buy-in. In other words, they have freedom to do this because of their track record of implementing well.

As mentioned earlier in this book, ideas need time to develop. One of the most practical ways to develop an idea is simply to write it down. I know it sounds elementary, but it really is one of the most important things you can do to get an idea off the ground. Here's how it helps:

- **Writing forces you to articulate your concept.** Have you ever seen the look of sheer confusion or uninterest in the face of a person to whom you were trying to explain an idea? A major cause of this disconnect can be traced back to our own lack of clarity around an idea (even when it's our own!).

- **Writing can refine your idea by helping you see both its strengths and weaknesses.** It provides a canvas upon which you can edit and even track the evolution of a thought. It will often open up more options and pathways to consider.

- **Writing your concept down creates a point of reference for conversations about your idea with others.** In addition, it allows you to converse with yourself by providing you a fictive third-person perspective.

- **Writing your idea down makes it more shareable.** You can send your document to others without you having to always be present. It can create its own opportunities.

Jack Dorsey, cofounder of Twitter and chief executive officer (CEO) of Square, views his role as an editor of ideas and teams. I've heard him speak on a handful of occasions where he has emphasized the importance of revisiting ideas and continually editing them in order to produce a better product and company.[1]

Ideas need continual editing, and this is not possible if we don't write things down. A purely verbal idea culture without any documentation is going to be extremely difficult, if not impossible, to sustain long term. Serious idea makers regularly write things down. In fact, most of them write before speaking so that they can more clearly communicate the true essence of their ideas.

I think we all know people who talk a lot about new ideas. They talk, talk, talk, and then talk some more. Unfortunately, many of their ideas have never seen the light of day. Tragically, with each new idea they talk

---

[1]For Jack Dorsey's thoughts on editing, see www.PSFK.com/2011/06/twitters-jack-dorsey-on-ceo-as-editor.html#ixzz1SbXR05qX.

about, they lose credibility with those who experience fatigue with each new great idea. Can't you see the eyes rolling?

Have a good idea? Make sure you take the time to write it down before you share it. We want to be supportive of your idea, but we need to know if you know what you're asking for.

Good Idea (key thoughts from this section)	Now What? (your ideas and next steps for execution)
People who have a tendency to share their ideas immediately, without any sense of process, are probably less likely to actually implement their ideas.	_____ _____ _____
One of the most practical ways to develop an idea is simply to write it down.	_____ _____ _____
Writing can help you see both your idea's strengths and weaknesses. Do it!	_____ _____ _____

CHAPTER
24

Think Multiple, Not Perfect

I have the perfect recipe!

A few years back, I came across a TED[1] talk video of noted author and speaker Malcolm Gladwell speaking about spaghetti sauce. Quite honestly, the title hooked me into watching it (along with the fact that I like most things Malcolm Gladwell has to say). Little did I know that this video would radically change the way I think about problem solving.

Malcolm Gladwell shared the story of Howard Moskowitz, a brilliant consultant to some of the largest brands in the world. Back in the early 1970s, Pepsi-Cola came to Moskowitz to seek his help in finding the perfect Diet Pepsi. As one would expect, Moskowitz facilitated multiple taste groups in hopes of finding the most popular concentration and mix of ingredients for Diet Pepsi. Most food and drink companies during that time simply took the most popular feedback from taste tests to produce their products. Unfortunately for Moskowitz, the data did not return a nice bell curve of opinion. Instead, the data revealed that there were no dominant preferences from the taste groups.

Most other people in the food industry at the time would have taken a data set like this and then proceeded to make an educated guess as to what might be best. Moskowitz was no ordinary consultant. He was not intellectually satisfied with these unusual data. Moskowitz continued

---

[1]TED is a conference that brings together people from three different worlds: technology, entertainment, and design. In recent years, its scope has broadened with its ever-growing global presence. You can view videos of their talks at www.TED.com.

to wrestle with this quandary for a few years until one day, while sitting at a diner doing some work for Nescafé, the answer hit him like a bolt of lightning. He realized that he had been asking the wrong question. Instead of asking, "What is the perfect Diet Pepsi?" he should have been asking, "What are the perfect Diet Pepsis?"

Moskowitz realized that looking for the Platonic ideal for a Diet Pepsi recipe was the wrong focus. Rather, he should have been looking for clusters in the data to identify the perfect recipes for Diet Pepsi. Moskowitz began to share this new thought at his speaking engagements as he traveled around the country. Unfortunately, very few people understood what he was talking about. Nevertheless, Moskowitz continued to propagate this new way of thinking.

After a few years, Campbell Soup, who made Prego, hired Moskowitz to help them find the perfect recipe for spaghetti sauce. Some of you may not remember this, but during the 1970s and early 1980s, there was only one kind of spaghetti sauce: plain. It was commonly believed that the best kind of spaghetti sauce was that which was closest to the original (i.e., the kind made in Italy). Of course, Moskowitz did not take this approach. Instead, he went on a pursuit to find the perfect sauces for Prego. Moskowitz had thousands of people taste test 45 varieties of spaghetti sauce!

The data that came back showed that people fell into one of the following three taste clusters:

1. Plain or traditional

2. Spicy

3. Extra chunky

Prego was thoroughly surprised by the third cluster identified. In response, they quickly created a new line of spaghetti sauce that was extra chunky. Over the next 10 years, extra chunky spaghetti sauce made the company more than $600 million.

Soon afterward, many other companies, including Ragu (Prego's main competitor), hired Moskowitz to help them find perfect recipes. Pretty soon, everyone from mustard companies to coffee companies followed suit. How many versions of a product do you now see at your local grocery store? Howard Moskowitz has brought a lot of happiness to all of us food lovers.

Spaghetti Sauce Lessons

What does this have to do with ideas?

I think the big insight I walked away with was to shift my thinking from finding the perfect solution to a need or problem to looking for multiple solutions. Instead of asking myself, "What is the perfect way to do this?" I began to ask myself, "What are the perfect ways to do this?" This slight (but major) shift in thinking opened up many new creative ways of approaching ideas.

You see, there are no Platonic, universal solutions for ideas. Each idea is unique and therefore requires us to think in terms of multiple pathways and solutions. Idea makers should consider developing multiple ways to accomplish the task rather than stressing to find the perfect way. In fact, the pathway to actualizing your idea will rarely, if ever, be the pathway you intended at the beginning. Fluidity is an essential element to planning. This doesn't negate planning; it frames the environment for refining plans along the way.

For example, lately many clients have asked our company whether they should allocate the majority of their marketing funds to social media, especially in light of its popularity. My answer: it's the wrong question. You have to think multiple platforms and solutions. Social media is just one of the ways that people can connect with your work—not the only way. It may be a perfect recipe for some, but not all. Finding how it fits into your overall marketing plan is a much better way to look at it.

In the same way, trying to find the best way of providing customer service for a business may be the wrong way to look at the problem. Consider reframing the question to open up a new world of possibilities.

Good Idea (key thoughts from this section)	Now What? (your ideas and next steps for execution)
Shift your thinking from looking for the one perfect solution to a need or problem to finding multiple solutions.	
The pathway to actualizing your idea will rarely, if ever, be the pathway you intended at the beginning.	

Taking It Further

What answers do you think you need to have before you can start moving forward with your idea? Write them down. Now revisit the list and cross out all that you can't honestly say you *must* know the answer *with 100% certainty*.

Review the list of characteristics of an idea maker in Chapter 21. Which of those describe you?

What data would help you gain an advantage in your field? List the key phrases that describe those data. Do an online search for those phrases and see what you can learn.

If you haven't already done so, take time now to write down your idea. Now share it with a trusted friend to see if he or she understands your concept. Is it clear and compelling?

What simple act can you take to get you started toward your goal? Do it today. Tell someone else so that person can hold you accountable.

Elements for Idea Making 2

Simple

Water. Clean, safe water.

One in eight people on our planet don't have access to clean, safe drinking water. It is estimated that unsafe water and a lack of basic sanitation cause 80 percent of all disease and kill more people in our world than all forms of violence combined.

Clean, safe water changes everything.

Building wells, irrigation systems, latrines, hand-washing stations, and rainwater collection tanks can significantly change the life of a community. In addition to significantly reducing the amount of waterborne diseases, water creates everything from educational opportunities for kids who would otherwise spend most of their days fetching water to gender equality for women who now have leadership positions within a village as they help manage new water sources.

Scott Harrison saw this firsthand while traveling in Africa as a humanitarian photographer with the medical relief organization Mercy Ships. He documented thousands of people who had been affected by unsafe water. Scott learned from water experts that there were viable solutions to the crisis. The problem could be solved.

Upon returning to the United States, Scott started an organization in New York called charity: water. Its mission? Bring clean, safe drinking water to people in developing countries. He began to tell the story of water to everyone around him who would listen. Scott organized gallery showings of his photographs that told the story, and he built interactive water exhibitions throughout the city so that people could see the reality of the water crisis.

He and his team began selling $20 bottles of water—the cost of bringing clean water to someone overseas. These creative ideas quickly gained the support of individual donors, major brands, and multiple media outlets.

In the first five years of its existence, charity: water, with the help of more than 200,000 donors worldwide, has raised more than $40 million to run the organization, launch educational campaigns, and fund water projects. To date, charity: water has funded nearly 4,000 water projects, providing access to clean, safe drinking water for more than 2 million people in 19 countries.

Scott and his team have worked incredibly hard to clearly communicate their message and to offer bite-sized ways for anyone interested in helping out to get involved. Their branding and marketing mirrors something that looks like it came out of Madison Avenue. Could a not-for-profit organization have such a strong brand? Most definitely!

In a recent conversation with Scott, I asked him how charity: water keeps their message so clear and simple. He told me that his team has a natural bent toward simplicity. Scott proceeded to clarify what he meant by this. He said that most people on his team naturally look for ways to simplify an idea. Still, to keep things simple, one must be comfortable with the complexities of business. Scott believes that making things simple requires a wealth of knowledge and understanding.

Whether it's in the area of marketing, business strategy, or technology, having a wide breadth of knowledge creates the clarity needed to produce something simply remarkable.

As long as I've known Scott, he's been a consummate learner. He leverages the knowledge of others through intentional relationships to help him in specific areas of need along the way. It's no wonder that his organization continues to lead the way in creative innovation for human good.

Many of the memorable ideas in our world were the result of knowledgeable people working hard toward simplicity. Simplifying an idea by removing unnecessary conceptual extensions is a skill that must be nurtured by any idea maker. This is not to say that ideas aren't complex. Rather, simplicity is a virtue that allows for complex concepts to be clearly communicated and easily understood. It may be the determining factor in whether someone comes on board and supports your idea.

Good idea makers believe in regularly editing ideas down to their core essence. They recognize that removing a feature is sometimes more important than adding one. Identifying the core of an idea also opens up creative opportunities for other people to adapt the concept for greater effectiveness. Simple ideas such as Twitter and PayPal have facilitated the creation and growth of numerous companies and organizations.

Simplifying an idea is hard work—and, it's essential to creating quality and ensuring scalability. Here are some questions that may help you keep your ideas simple:

- What is the core concept that my idea is founded upon?
- What elements of the idea are essential to its launch and/or success?
- What distinguishes this idea from others in the category?
- Can I edit the idea down?
- Will the new feature that's being introduced help or hurt the concept?
- Is the idea clear and bite-sized enough for someone to want to listen and choose to participate?
- Can I succinctly communicate the idea to someone who has no context for the concept?

Good Idea (key thoughts from this section)	Now What? (your ideas and next steps for execution)
A wide breadth of knowledge creates the clarity needed to produce something simply remarkable.	
Many of the memorable ideas in our world were the result of knowledgeable people working hard toward simplicity.	
Identifying the core of an idea opens up creative opportunities for other people to adapt the concept for greater effectiveness.	

Quality, Quality, Quality

"Fake it until you make it."

In years past, advertisers and marketers were able to dress up subpar products and make them look stellar in the public eye. They used great design, clever messaging, and strategic placement to lure potential customers. The lack of peer-to-peer communication and access to information limited consumers' ability to voice their thoughts about a product.

How times have changed!

The growth of the Internet, with its socially driven user reviews, has changed the game when it comes to identifying quality products or services. In our networked culture, instant and public feedback on consumer experience has become the norm. People will post thoughts, pictures, videos, and blogs about a product or service within seconds of experiencing it. In fact, most people will do their research—comparing prices, reviews, and options—prior to ever trying your new offering.

Quality matters.

Whether you're selling products or services, we now live in an age in which we will not be able to fake quality. The good news if your company focuses on quality is that your story will be told. People will publicly share their positive experiences with your brand and tell your story. This will often lead to brand loyalty and repeat business.

Quality wins.

As a consultant, I travel quite a bit each month. One of the natural by-products of my vocation is that you become more particular about travel comfort and the quality of hospitality-related services. I'm always willing to pay a little more if it means that I can alleviate the wear and tear on my body. I also appreciate people who take the few extra minutes of effort to provide better service. I automatically become loyal to their brands.

Rick Ueno is the general manager of Sheraton Chicago. Under his leadership these past five years, Sheraton Chicago has significantly improved its employee and guest satisfaction ratings, profitability, and market share. They have also risen to become one of the best convention hotels for Sheraton in the country.

I was introduced to Rick through a mutual friend over breakfast at the Sheraton. Rick invited me to stay at the Sheraton whenever I found myself in Chicago for client work (which was once a month at the time). I had been there for a conference several years back and didn't remember anything special about my stay. Nevertheless, I appreciated the invite and booked a stay there for my next trip.

Upon my arrival at the Sheraton the next month, I was completely impressed by the quality of service provided by Rick and his staff. I entered my room to find a note, handwritten by Rick, welcoming me to his hotel. In addition, he had prepped his staff to deliver a nice tray of snacks to the room. Later, Rick followed up with a phone call to make sure everything was good with my stay. They had me. I was sold. Their pricing was fair, and their service was superior.

I have since returned to the Sheraton many times. The accommodations of the hotel are great, and the coordinated efforts of the staff have been nothing less than five star. Over the last several months of going back, I've begun some great conversations with Rick about how he is creating a work culture that continues to raise the level of quality. He graciously offered the following principles for developing a culture that values high quality:

- **Quality necessitates a commitment to experimentation and learning.** Rick and his team are regularly experimenting and trying out new ideas. Whether it's redesigning the lobby, refining the check-in process, or reimagining event productions, Rick has created space for his team to be creative. He feeds this culture of experimentation by providing ongoing opportunities for his team to continue learning through books, professional training, and team-driven conversations. Rick is regularly recognized in his industry as a leading innovator in hotel management.

- **Quality embraces accountability.** Delegating tasks from the top down is ineffective in Rick's opinion. He believes that creating a highly accountable system of checks and balances is necessary to ensure quality. Rick doesn't engage in big brother micromanaging, but he is completely committed to making sure everyone stays true to their word and follows through. Most of his meetings are action-oriented and require the participation of everyone on the team to report on their follow-up items from the previous meeting. Rick expects people to do their work and doesn't feel the need to be mean or disrespectful in asking for accountability. Rick is neither shy in confronting someone, without making things personal, nor slow in affirming the work of his team. He has developed a process of follow-up via calendar and task reminders on his phone that allow him to stay on top of his game. Rick shared that working hard on a process of mini-milestones, self-policing systems, and regular team updates has made life easier for everyone involved.

- **Quality is the result of collaborative work.** Rick rarely does anything on his own. He believes in working in committees because it allows people to participate and creates new learning opportunities. Rick's approach to empowering teams rather than controlling their decisions has birthed fresh ideas and a group of individuals passionate about implementing well.

- **Quality of work is strengthened by quality of life outside of work.** Rick's team works hard—very hard. But it's not just about working hard. Rick recognizes that a healthful life outside of work is essential to productivity in the office. He regularly encourages his team to develop an enjoyable life outside of work. Work isn't everything for Rick. He works hard to model this value in the way he embraces life as a whole. Rick usually has a big smile on his face when he's working on site as well as when it's time to go home.

People like Rick remind me that working on quality doesn't have to be grueling. It's a process that can be enjoyed thoroughly. Working on something you are passionate about should be an act of love. As you continue to focus on developing quality, don't forget to enjoy the journey.

Here are some additional thoughts and questions that help me stay focused on quality when working on ideas:

- **Be honest about progress.** There's no use in being dishonest about how well an idea is developing when people ask. Being upfront with challenges allows others to help you develop your idea. Also, it will prevent you from overpromising and creating unrealistic expectations.

- **Who determines what quality is?** Is there a standard of measurement? How will you determine your metrics for quality?

- **What are the nonnegotiable areas for quality?** Remember, the goal is not to have the perfect product or service. In fact, all great ideas are works in progress. Nevertheless, you should have a good grasp on which foundational elements of your idea must be in place for an idea to flourish.

- **Seek outside voices.** Like so many other areas of idea development, inviting input from those outside the project at several key milestones can help greatly. This is not to say that you must listen to all new input, but key feedback moments can help you evaluate how you are progressing. Keep the objectives of your project in mind whenever you're asking for feedback on quality. Some feedback may seem great, but it may be irrelevant to your project's goals.

Good Idea (key thoughts from this section)	Now What? (your ideas and next steps for execution)
Quality necessitates a commitment to experimentation and learning.	
A healthful life outside of work is essential to productivity in the office.	
Working on something you are passionate about should be an act of love.	

CHAPTER

27

The F Word

"That's an amazing idea!"

"Thanks!"

"How do you plan to fund it?"

"Well . . . I'm hoping . . . I think my friends will help . . ."

This is an all too common conversation I've had with numerous founders of start-ups or new ventures. Many idea lovers spend the majority of their time thinking about the creative elements of an idea rather than developing a business plan for implementation that includes a strategic plan for funding the endeavor.

I completely understand why this happens. It is usually far more energizing and interesting to think about the creative development of an idea than it is to think about the funding. Unfortunately, ideas can't survive on creativity alone. They usually need the backing of cold, hard cash. The last time I checked, ideas alone can't pay the bills. Sooner or later, idea makers will have to come to grips with how they plan to fund an idea.

I always feel like a party pooper when I bring this up—but I always prefer to deal with the poop now rather than wait and let it hit the fan.

In many cases, the conversation of funding will involve looking into outside sources for investment or support. Although I completely agree that bootstrapping and not taking outside funding may be the best option, there may be moments in the life of a company or organization that necessitate the integration of outside fiscal help. In these moments, it's vital to have a good approach to engaging potential funders.

For example, funding has very little to do with simply getting money for a project. It's far more relational and collaborative than many would think. Asking for funding is essentially inviting someone to partner with you on an endeavor at a very tangible level. In fact, the exchange of money is only part of the transaction. The goal of funding is not the money transaction, but rather the mutual benefits of an ongoing relationship. If managed well, that relationship will continue to yield returns on multiple levels. Funding is just one of the by-products of relationship.

When it comes to funding an idea, the first name that comes to mind is my good friend Keith Kall.

Keith is the senior director of global corporate partnerships at World Vision, one of the largest nonprofit organizations in the world. He spends most of his time building joint-equity partnerships and alliances with Fortune 1000 companies in order to improve health, economic opportunities, and overall quality of life for impoverished families and communities in Africa, Asia, and Latin America. Prior to joining World Vision, Keith helped successfully expand multiple companies' networks, portfolios, and campaigns by developing relationally driven networks that facilitated mutually beneficial opportunities for investors and groups seeking collaboration. It's no wonder that I often turn to him for insights in this area.

During one of our regular lunch meet-ups, I asked him to articulate some of the principles that guide his thinking while meeting with potential funders. Here is a synopsis of some of Keith's insights:

- **Information is key. Do your homework.** We live in a world where we have instant access to a seemingly infinite amount of information. Before entering a meeting with a potential funder, always do your homework. Commit to becoming well versed in the passions and interests of the person or company you are seeking to partner with. You should have a clear picture of why and how the collaboration may work. Whether you choose to do online searches or speak with people who have had prior connections to the person(s) you're meeting with, the key is that you enter the meeting with a deep sense of confidence about that person's work.

- **Ask a lot of questions and listen well.** Since the goal is mutual benefit through relational collaboration, view the meeting as an opportunity to interview a potential partner for your endeavor. In other words, you are not there to simply pitch an idea in hopes of receiving funds. The goal is not a transaction, but a relationship. It's all about the relationship. You're there to find the right people to work with on your idea. Don't be shy in asking questions and taking great notes. Focus on listening proactively by asking relevant follow-up questions that provide clarity regarding a possible partnership. If you have done your homework, you should already have a list of questions ready for engagement, and each question should guide you closer to or farther from a potential partnership.

- **Think of the other party's interest and offer to help.** If you're seeking to build a lasting partnership, the interaction can't be unilateral. It can't be about convincing the person on the other side of the table to help you out. Rather, view it as an opportunity to come around and sit on the same side of the table. Asking a simple question such as, "How can I help you in your efforts?" can really change the relational dynamics of the engagement. This will often open up a world of creative opportunities for further collaboration.

- **Identify, articulate, and marry interests.** Both parties involved should walk away feeling that they have found mutual benefit and a stronger relationship. This requires us to identify and articulate the areas in which our interests can marry the interests of the other party. Communicating verbally during the meeting and then following up afterward in written form can help bring clarity and direction.

- **Don't always try to close the deal on the first date.** Relationships take time to develop. There's no need to rush the deal during your first meeting. In fact, give yourself permission not to pursue the deal any further if you don't feel it's a fit. Remember, money alone can't be the sole criterion for partnership. It should feel like a courtship. Take your time, follow its pace, and wait for a deep sense of peace about working together. This will provide far more benefits in the long run. However, if it's love at first sight, go for it!

Funding is a great avenue to developing long-lasting relationships. It carries a lot of weight because it's so essential to making an idea come alive. It's truly an invitation to an intimate journey. Never take it lightly. In addition, taking time to develop an approach to funding will help you further scale your idea.

Build a strategy that creates multiple pathways for people to get involved and develop a strong sense of brand identification or ownership.

Funding is most definitely a great pathway for involvement. It can be the difference between a nice idea and an idea that becomes reality.

Good Idea (key thoughts from this section)	Now What? (your ideas and next steps for execution)
Ideas alone can't pay the bills. Sooner or later, idea makers will have to come to grips with how they plan to fund an idea.	_____ _____ _____
Asking someone for funding is essentially inviting that person to partner with you on an endeavor at a very tangible level.	_____ _____ _____
There's no need to rush to close the deal during your first meeting. Take it slow and wait for a deep sense of peace about working together.	_____ _____ _____

Under Pressure

I love New York.

Although I have spent the majority of my life living in Southern California, there has always been a place in my heart for the city I first immigrated to. It's a city full of vibrancy, vitality, and unparalleled tenacity to endure life's greatest challenges. It is by far my favorite city to visit. I love walking around Manhattan, admiring the diversity of people, tastes, and styles. The hustle and bustle of the city always reminds me that the world is continuing to move forward. You can almost get a glimpse of the future in a city like New York.

Frank Sinatra was right. It's the city that never sleeps. It's ever working, ever playing, and ever dreaming of a better tomorrow.

It's no wonder that I jump at most opportunities to work with clients in New York. I often walk away inspired by clients who do so much with so much at stake in the midst of so many expectations. The reality is that you can't fake it in New York. The pressure cooker environment will either catapult you into greatness or eat you alive.

During a recent business trip to New York, my colleague and I had the privilege of shadowing and interviewing Soledad O'Brien for a day while working on a project for her. As many know, Soledad is one of the premier news correspondents at CNN and the lead for many of CNN's top documentaries about America. More impressively, she is also the mother of four beautiful children and happily married to Brad Raymond. If there's anyone who understands the pressures that surround idea making, it's Soledad.

I was awestruck by the number of projects, amount of travel, and real-time pressure that surrounded her daily activities at CNN. Nevertheless, I sensed a great calm and focus in Soledad's life that guided her through what appeared to be ever-increasing demands and expectations. I was thoroughly impressed by her ability to pause throughout the day to interact with team members, fans online, and even strangers on the street. In each instance, she was fully present when engaging people.

Soledad invited us over that night to her home so that we could meet her husband and her kids. I was deeply encouraged to see her give each of her children undivided attention during her conversations with them. There was plenty of laughter and a great sense of joy in that home. I could see in the faces of her children that they knew their mom was accessible and engaged. I was challenged at that moment to develop a similar environment in my own home. What a great model for work and family!

During a recent phone call, I asked her how she works so well under pressure—something that most idea makers will have to learn. Soledad didn't hesitate and instinctively responded, "It's not that difficult." She continued to share the following four principles that help her lead a healthful and enjoyable life amid the pressure:

- **Go back to your guiding life principles.** These are principles, both personal and professional, that establish a foundation for day-to-day decision making. For example, as a news correspondent, Soledad lives by the principle that one should never ambush the person(s) being interviewed. Soledad prides herself in doing her best to research and develop relevant questions for her interviews. This principle keeps her from being distracted by the temptation to corner someone or press into areas that aren't appropriate or related to her story. Another life principle for Soledad is that one ought to enjoy the process and journey of life even more than its destination. You can definitely see this in her interactions with people and her uncanny ability to pause and enjoy the presence of another. It's clear that people take precedence over projects and purpose over momentary pleasure.

- **Winnow down to what really matters.** Soledad is committed to making sure that she pursues only opportunities that resonate with the path she wants her life to take. Working on things that are meaningful, even if it is more difficult, is far better than settling for the comfortable and familiar. At the end of the day, she is a firm believer that we ought to work on things that really matter.

- **Use visuals to step back and get a clearer picture.** Soledad shared with me her reliance on visuals for her work. For example, she mentioned how practical it is to have a calendar, both printed and digital, that provides a bird's-eye view of all of her projects. Regularly taking a step back to physically view her calendar gives her a better sense of what it will take to deliver well. Soledad believes that a visual of the process and progress is essential to making sure things get done.

- **Work around your weaknesses and gather a great team.** Soledad is a person of deep self-awareness. She will be the first one to tell you what she is good at as well as those areas she needs help in. Soledad believes that making stuff up to fill the void of needed expertise will eventually backfire. Taking the time to develop a team around one's weakness is a must for idea makers. Teamwork is key to great ideas coming alive.

There is no doubt the demands and deadlines of our vocational pursuits can often become quite overwhelming. The reality is that pressure will never go away. But, as Soledad models well, pressure does not have to stifle or suffocate our dreams.

In addition to Soledad's insights, the following principles and approaches for working under pressure are also useful:

- **Get started and don't argue.** I used to find myself spending too much time arguing with myself about whether I could meet the expectations and/or deadlines of a project. The complexity of the projects set before me used to cause a mental (and sometimes physical) paralysis. I soon realized that this inner battle only wasted time. I decided to just jump in, even without all the information or strategy. I've discovered that the key to getting things done starts with a simple act toward a goal. Risky? Possibly. Productive? Most definitely. It sounds so elementary, but doing something is better than not doing anything.

- **Set mini-deadlines/milestones.** Breaking down larger deadlines into smaller, bite-sized milestones can really help you move forward. Yes, it's probably impossible to determine all of your smaller milestones at the beginning of a project, but nonetheless, moving in this direction will give you significant momentum and hope. Project management software helps a lot as well if you're willing to utilize it. (*Hint:* You probably need to find some software or system that helps you keep things on track. It will be well worth your time and investment.) Taking the time at the beginning to schedule your milestones can save your sanity, time over the long run, and help you formulate a great work pace.

- **Get off social media and e-mails when possible.** Although I am a firm believer in the power and usefulness of social media and e-mail, I also recognize that these can be one of the greatest deterrents to getting stuff done. Blocking off a few hours to work on a project without access to these tools will often produce some of your greatest results. If you need to answer e-mails, set a specific time and work within those parameters. I've realized that setting aside specific times for e-mail has actually allowed me to answer more e-mails because I've learned that I work better with smaller segments of time with specific tasks.

- **Find your work rhythm.** Recognizing when you are most creative or alert can really increase productivity. For example, if you are most focused and productive in the morning, schedule the heaviest creative work during that time. Don't schedule work that may not best use your personal work rhythm. In other words, mornings in this scenario may not be the best time to answer e-mail or attend a project update meeting. Chapter 16 is dedicated to this principle.

- **Exercise and eat well.** Countless studies have shown the correlation between physical health and ability to work under pressure. (Ouch, I know.) I'm not saying that you have to be a gym rat to be productive. It might be as simply as going for a brisk walk after a meal for 10 minutes to get your blood flowing again or choosing healthier meal options at lunch. Staying healthy can make a world of difference.

Good Idea (key thoughts from this section)	Now What? (your ideas and next steps for execution)
Pressure will never go away, but pressure does not have to stifle or suffocate our dreams or our relationships that matter to us.	_____ _____ _____
Making stuff up to fill the void of needed expertise will eventually backfire. Taking the time to develop a team around one's weakness is a must for idea makers.	_____ _____ _____
The key to getting things done starts with a simple act toward a goal. Doing something is better than not doing anything.	_____ _____ _____

CHAPTER
29

Dealing with Setbacks

Yes, most idea makers will experience setbacks.
Whether it's due to our lack of ability to plan properly or simply life happenings outside of our control, unforeseen circumstances will become a constant reality for idea makers. The only predictable thing in life may be that life is unpredictable.

Once we come to the place of acknowledging that setbacks are a part of the idea-making process, I think we will be better prepared to deal with them.

Changing the World through Shoes

In 2006, Blake Mycoskie was traveling in Argentina when he came across children in poverty who were unable to afford shoes. Blake soon discovered that soil-transmitted diseases, which can penetrate the skin through bare feet, were among the most prevalent diseases in developing countries. In addition to providing physical protection, shoes also provide children with the ability to attend school, because most schools require shoes as part of their uniform.

Blake came back to the United States and rallied his friends and family to donate 10,000 pairs of shoes to the children of Argentina by the end of that year. He also decided to start a company called TOMS.[1] The business model for TOMS is simple: for every pair of shoes purchased, TOMS gives a pair of shoes to a child in need.

---

[1]For more information on TOMS, visit www.TomsShoes.com.

In the short time of its existence, TOMS has given away more than 1 million shoes in over 20 countries. TOMS are sold in hundreds of stores nationwide, and the company continues to scale greatly. It has been featured on numerous news outlets, blogs, and commercials, including one by AT&T that propelled its exposure and buy-in from the general public.

With this kind of success, many would assume that TOMS has everything together and going for them. This is definitely somewhat true. Blake runs a great company that is committed to excellence in all that it does. Nevertheless, the company is not immune to unexpected obstacles and potential setbacks. What distinguishes TOMS is its ability to honestly engage and improve when obstacles arise.

In a recent conversation with Blake, I asked how he and his team continue to improve and work through setbacks. Blake quickly pointed out that a company is only as strong as its weakest link. As TOMS began to scale quickly, with new opportunities constantly presenting themselves, Blake and his team were faced with the reality that their shoe production could not keep up with the demand. They quickly had to scale production, customer service, and distribution infrastructure. TOMS sought external advice while increasing internal staffing. Experiences like these have also created a preventive culture in which they are regularly looking to strengthen the weakest areas of their company.

Blake also shared with me that he has learned to not panic and to keep things in perspective when setbacks arise. He noted that all things pass away and many things that feel big in the moment often end up not being a big deal at all within a few weeks. As a leader, he recognizes that panic does not aid in problem solving, nor does it provide any direction to a team wanting to move forward.

I think TOMS will continue to be successful because of their commitment to move forward in the midst of obstacles and setbacks. It's nonnegotiable. TOMS has already predetermined that it will be an action-oriented, solutions-based company.

When dealing with life's unexpected curveballs, the following ideas will prove useful:

- **Choose optimism.** As mentioned earlier, some circumstances will be out of your control. This means that there's nothing you can do to change the past. Move forward. There may be some assessment that needs to take place about what didn't work, but assess while moving forward. No matter how disheartening the setback may be, choose optimism. Pessimism will only paralyze and depress you. Also, be sure to surround yourself with other optimists who can be constructive and encouraging.

- **Think opportunity.** History tells us that some of the greatest idea makers (e.g., Edison, Lincoln, Disney, Jobs, and Gates) all had major setbacks while pursuing their dreams. They chose to view those obstacles as opportunities to improve their ideas. They knew that what they were working for was too important to allow setbacks to derail them from achieving their ideas. Every setback produces new opportunities. Who knows? The setback may be exactly what you need to take your idea to the next level!

- **Recalibrate.** A setback is just that . . . a setback. Recalibrate your approach. Think of setbacks as detours toward discovering a better future. If you're going to fall momentarily, fall forward. May your new perspective from the ground give you a renewed vision for your idea. Take a deep breath and get back up. The character and tenacity you build during these setbacks will ultimately set a great foundation for a lifetime of great work.

- **Don't be too hard on yourself.** Although there are always things that could have been done better, try not to be too hard on yourself. Your life is *not* over! Keep in mind that many ideas take more than just the willingness and planning of one person to make it work. Ideas also involve timing, teamwork, and unexpected resources. A setback doesn't necessarily mean that you had a bad idea.

I like what my friend Brad Lomenick told me recently about pressure and setbacks. Brad leads Catalyst, one of the largest networks of young leaders in our country, and says:

If it's not life threatening, it's not that big of a deal. It's going to be okay. You're not that big of a deal. Relax. (Oh yeah, this one really hit home.)

People like you, who are committed to living out your ideas, inspire me. As one who experiences these setbacks regularly, I want to encourage you to keep moving forward. Your ideas can change our world for the better, so don't give up!

Good Idea (key thoughts from this section)	Now What? (your ideas and next steps for execution)
Unforeseen circumstances are a constant reality for idea makers. The only predictable thing in life may be that life is unpredictable.	_____ _____ _____
All things pass away, and many things that feel big in the moment often end up not being a big deal at all within a few weeks.	_____ _____ _____
Panic does not aid in problem solving, nor does it provide any direction to a team wanting to move forward.	_____ _____ _____
Every setback provides new opportunities.	_____ _____

CHAPTER

30

Beat the Tribal Drum

A school of fish.
A herd of cattle.
A pack of wolves.
A band of brothers.
Groupon. (Just kidding.)

We were designed to move through life together, as a tribe. A tribe is a group of committed individuals united by a common purpose, interest, or kinship that seeks to journey together for greater strength and impact.

Tribes can shape personal preferences, cultural trends, and even worldviews. Whether it's an idea, a product, or a cause, a tribe can catapult something or someone to a new level of influence. A tribe has the power to dictate who becomes a celebrity, drive record-breaking sales, or even get someone elected as president. Brand loyalty is often the result of a tribal buy-in and participation.

Forming and leading a tribe is one of the greatest privileges a person can experience. It's quite an honor to be identified as a tribal leader for a movement, because a tribe is not simply a group of casual followers. It's a family of people who are willing to go out of their way to support who you are and what you do.

Over the past few years, I've had the privilege of developing and leading a handful of tribal communities in their infancy. These tribes have centered on different interests, including social good, entrepreneurism, and idea making. The paradoxical truth about tribal leadership is that the tribe must bestow leadership upon you. You need the tribe to recognize

129

your credibility and genuine commitment to the greater good of everyone involved. It can't be forced. Leadership often arises in the midst of serving others. Nevertheless, here are some practical principles for intentionally developing a healthy tribe around your idea:

- **Tribes need focus and clarity.** Leading a tribe requires the clear communication of why the tribe exists in the first place and what it uniquely brings to the table. A lack of clarity will result in a lack of commitment that ultimately will dilute anything you are trying to build. What is your tribe about, and why does it need to exist? Why should I care about what you're inviting me to?

  Be clear in communicating tribal goals and expectations. The whole world can't be your tribe. There must be some distinctive qualities that are publicly recognized and regularly reiterated by its members.

- **Tribes grow one person and one story at a time.** Relationships still matter. The human story is what builds a tribe and cuts through the white noise of marketing. Although social media, networking, and marketing may help get the word out about your tribe, it is the human sell (i.e., the sharing and embodying of the tribe's message from one person to another) that will make it remarkable. People are bombarded with advertisements around the clock. The stories about your tribe from those within it will often be one of the best avenues for marketing what you're about. In other words, focus on each individual who cared enough to believe in you and your efforts. Take time to thank your tribe—one by one if possible. Celebrate and platform each member. Invite them to build the tribe with you and find practical ways to empower their ability to do so. Regularly take time to listen to the ideas of those within the tribe and create pathways for tribal involvement. Never underestimate the power of one voice. Regardless of its size, the tribe's power will always reside in human relationships.

- **Tribes still need good leadership.** Tribes aren't built on cruise control. Most tribes that have been effective in our world have had strong leadership. Whether it's an individual or a team, the work of leading a tribe is just that—work. More specifically, it's intentional and intelligent work. Someone needs to spend time building a tribe. Facilitating growth and loyalty requires ongoing relationship building.

- **Tribal leadership is more about facilitation and less about control.** Tribal leaders understand that control is not the goal of community.

Rather, the goal is to facilitate an environment in which the community may live out its mission and purpose. Cultural architecture is key to developing a vibrant tribe. Instead of focusing on how to control members, tribal leaders focus on creating a culture in which people joining will naturally sense the personality, ethos, and mission of the group. Those who don't embrace the tribal culture will quickly find themselves disengaging and ultimately leaving. This is okay. Don't panic. In fact, it is for the best of those who *are* committed. Tribes need both insiders and outsiders. If not, there would be no basis for having a unique group.

- **Tribes can smell BS and will protect their own.** A vibrant tribe will often create its own checks and balances. It will quickly recognize the people who are genuine as well as those who are faking their way through or seeking to disrupt the movement. A tribe will often smell BS a mile away and find ways to deal with it on its own. Those who care about your tribe will rise to the occasion and work toward keeping the overall movement focused on its core values and mission.

  Wikipedia is a great example of this. When information is posted on an entry relevant to a tribe, members of that tribe are quick to correct the post or report it if necessary. Tribe members care deeply about the information being posted and shared. The leaders of Wikipedia have created a culture that gives permission to committed tribe members to police the information coming in. This kind of internal accountability has resulted in an information accuracy level that surpasses traditional encyclopedias.

- **Tribes naturally innovate.** Tribes will innovate by nature, constantly refining and improving. Opening up opportunities for your tribe will speed up creativity and implementation. To make this innovative culture a reality, you must trust your tribe. You must be willing to model the sharing of ideas and openness to contribution. Furthermore, there must be evidence that follow-up and tribal input are taken seriously. Without this relational equity, you will either end up managing the tribe or experiencing a mass exodus of people.

I believe that every good idea needs a tribe of people who believe in it and will advocate for it. As you'll see in our next section, good ideas usually don't happen alone.

Who are you leading, and why should they care?

Good Idea (key thoughts from this section)	Now What? (your ideas and next steps for execution)
Tribes can shape personal preferences, cultural trends, and even worldviews. Whether it's an idea, a product, or a cause, a tribe can catapult something or someone to a new level of influence.	_____
Regardless of its size, the tribe's power will always reside in human relationships.	_____
To create a culture of innovation, you must trust your tribe and model the sharing of ideas and openness to the contributions of others.	_____

Taking It Further

- Write down the core concept that your idea is founded upon. Which elements of your idea are essential to its success? Which are not? Edit your idea down to its simplest expression.
- Name three things you like to do outside of work. If you can't come up with three, you need to get a life! List three things you would like to try in the next month.
- What is your idea's most important, nonnegotiable metric for quality?
- If you are seeking funding for your idea, list the sources you are considering. How well do you know these people? Do you like them? Can you see reciprocal benefit by working together?
- Think of a recent setback you faced. Can you see any opportunities that emerged from it?
- What tribes do you belong to? What products or services has your tribe helped make popular or successful?

The Work of Collaboration

CHAPTER
31

Myths

E dison invented the lightbulb.
    Turning a computer on and off regularly is bad for it.
    Crunches are the best way to get a six-pack.
You shouldn't end a sentence with a preposition.
We only use 10 percent of our brains.
Myths.

Yes, these are all myths (i.e., unfounded beliefs that are widely accepted).

Myths sound reasonable from a distance and are rarely challenged. A myth is often accepted solely on the basis of its popularity or in blind trust of the one sharing it. Many myths are harmless and fun, but others can definitely mislead or construct a false view of the world.

I think there are several myths that surround the notion of collaboration (a.k.a. networking). It has become a catchword to throw around among people who feel that connecting has any value.

Although there's no doubt that individuals, organizations, and companies around the world are collaborating more than ever, it has also become clear that people using the word aren't necessarily referring to the same thing. Some use it far more casually than others. Some consider just staying in touch as collaboration, whereas others view collaboration as actual co-labor.

Take a moment to look at the word again. *Collaboration* contains within it the word *labor*, just like the word *networking* has the word *work* right in the middle of it. Collaboration is really about working together toward a common goal. As romantic as collaborating sounds, it takes a whole lot of intentional, proactive effort to do it well.

Executing ideas well often requires us to collaborate with others. Although this is not a difficult idea to sell, I think some of the following myths about collaboration subtly get in the way of developing meaningful partnerships.

Myth 1: Collaboration Just Happens on Its Own

This is the belief that collaborative efforts are the result of spontaneous relationships that come together at the right time. Although there is some truth to the fact that relationships do undergird many collaborative efforts, the reality is that these relationships need intentional building toward a common goal. Collaboration doesn't just happen. It requires initiation, trust, directional clarity, time, mutual understanding of expectations, resources, and an implementable plan to guide the process. Spontaneity can flow more freely when there's an understanding of what goes into collaboration.

Myth 2: Collaboration Is Intuitive for Everyone

I wish this was the case! Unfortunately, collaboration is not natural for everyone. Without clear guidelines for engagement, many will feel lost or confused about what is allowed and considered appropriate. Some need to feel a sense of permission and direction for interaction. Collaboration without guidelines is like playing a game without rules. It's highly unlikely that it will be productive or even enjoyable.

Myth 3: Collaboration Is an Act of Lightening the Workload

This view says that collaboration will lighten the workload just as delegation does. Unfortunately, this is usually not the case. Collaboration may rearrange responsibilities and areas of focus, but it doesn't necessarily lighten the amount of work. The beauty of collaboration is that it allows us to focus time and energy on our strengths while leaning more upon the specialty of others in their respective fields of expertise. It doesn't necessarily take away the quantity of work that needs to be accomplished.

In fact, it will probably lead to more hours of work since we will find ourselves working in areas of our passion. The good news is that collaboration often opens the door for more creative opportunities and avenues for greater impact.

Myth 4: Collaboration Is a One-Size-Fits-All Endeavor

Some people think that the collaborative process is consistent across all contexts and therefore is something you can jump right into when you're confident about the potential partnership. This couldn't be further from the truth. Each opportunity for collaboration will carry its own set of unique characteristics that should be carefully considered. For example, the way we collaborate among individuals can be quite different from the way that organizations collaborate with one another. Interdepartmental collaboration may carry a different set of nuances from business-to-business networking. There may be foundational values that drive your collaboration, but always stay flexible on how you plan to implement your vision.

Myth 5: Collaboration Is about Finding the Right Technological Tools

This perspective promotes the idea that in our digital age, technology is the primary vehicle through which individuals or groups can collaborate. Although I am a big fan of technology, most collaborative efforts require a significant investment of resources and time outside of technology, including face-to-face meetings. Simply finding the right technology tools is not enough. Quite honestly, many people have found the best tools but don't leverage them to assist them in their efforts. Technology can most definitely supplement collaborative projects, but it is insufficient in itself to provide all that is needed to work productively with others. Collaboration is both an online and offline endeavor.

■ ■ ■

These myths can distract us from the immense energy, inspiration, and productivity that await us when we collaborate well with others. Developing clear pathways through the clutter of these delusions will allow us to move further down the rail of execution. Collaboration is a necessity for most ideas. We need to figure out how to do it well.

Good Idea (key thoughts from this section)	Now What? (your ideas and next steps for execution)
Executing ideas well often requires us to collaborate with others.	_____ _____ _____
Collaboration doesn't just happen. It requires initiation, trust, directional clarity, time, mutual understanding of expectations, resources, and an imple- mentable plan to guide the process.	_____ _____ _____
Collaboration without guidelines is like playing a game without rules. It's highly unlikely that it will be productive or even enjoyable.	_____ _____ _____
Collaboration may rearrange responsibilities and areas of focus, but it doesn't necessarily lighten the amount of work.	_____ _____

CHAPTER

32

Human

The X Factor

Collaboration is both a mystery and a miracle.

It comes in all shapes, sizes, and textures. Collaboration is as unpredictable as the future and as ever changing as the wind. It lures us and dismisses without warning.

Collaboration is neither static nor guaranteed. Collaboration is truly a complex endeavor. It is complex because it involves complex beings— yes, people like you and me!

I've learned over the years that people are completely unpredictable. A person can be a great friend or partner one minute and then suddenly disconnect without much notice or reason. Others may start off as our worst enemies only to become some of our closest friends. Who knows why we act the way we do?

Crazy? Yes.

Surprising? Of course.

Unimaginable? Not really.

We're human. None of us have it all together, and all of us carry around deep, personal issues that create further complexity. We're all imperfect beings trying to find our way through life. It's no wonder that our involvement in collaboration makes it innately complex.

It's both a mystery and a miracle that we can work together for *any* extended period of time. Be sure to treasure those collaborative moments.

To collaborate well in these complex relationships, it's vitally important to remove the following obstacles:

- **Unclear Motives and Expectations:** Everyone comes into collaborative opportunities with their own set of expectations and motives for getting involved. This is quite natural. Interests are bound to differ in the parties entering a collaborative agreement.

  For example, a company may enter collaboration with the goal of thought refinement. In other words, the company wants to engage from time to time in an informal relationship that allows team members to share ideas and refine concepts for their company. Another company may enter a collaborative space in hopes of finding investment or partnership opportunities with long-term commitment in mind. Both parties could use the word *collaboration* and yet mean two totally different things.

  A practical way to minimize unnecessary complexity is to clearly state the kind of collaboration you think you are entering upfront, at the beginning of the relationship. Getting things down on paper, even if it's a simple one-sheet agreement, can make a world of difference. Minimally, you and the person(s) you are collaborating with will have a point of reference for conversation and potential refinement of arrangement.

  Have you ever left a meeting wondering what the other party was hoping to gain from the interaction with you? Have you ever left a meeting feeling that you did not clearly communicate your intent for engaging? When this is the case, it is highly unlikely that you will be able to move forward with any kind of real collaboration.

- **Unclear Roles:** Clarifying the roles of everyone involved is essential to great collaboration. This is something that should be articulated, agreed upon, and documented by those participating in the effort. Minimizing the he said/she said conversations will keep the project moving. I highly recommend that the parties involved designate a project manager who can oversee the entire, mutually agreed-upon process for engagement while keeping everyone accountable. Roles should also be tied to a clear understanding of milestones and expected deliverables. No matter how egalitarian an endeavor may *want* to be, it will still need people to take leadership in specific areas in order for the overall goal to become reality.

- **Unclear Metrics and Objectives:** How will you know if your collaborative effort was a success? What are the qualitative and quantitative metrics you will use to determine whether you've been successful? Are your metrics for success similar to those you are working with?

  Taking the time to write down the collective goals of a group will provide a tangible point of reference for everyone involved. Determine some mutually agreed-upon metrics to use to filter the success of an activity. The scope and depth of collaboration will often determine how extensive these metrics will be.

- **Unclear Follow-Up:** Many great ideas and opportunities fall by the wayside because of a person's or group's inability to follow up. It definitely feels a lot easier to promise to follow up in the future than to actually spend a few minutes after each meeting to do what you promised. Ironically, the longer you wait to follow up, the more difficult it will become—especially to do it well. Most of us will end up using lame excuses or blaming others to cover our inability to do what we promised. The problem is that most people can see right through the BS.

Here are some practical ways that I try to follow up with people I hope to collaborate with:

- I try to send an e-mail with a synopsis of the meeting within hours or minutes of talking. Some of this depends on my meeting schedule, but the general rule of thumb is that I need to communicate before any of us in the conversation forget. These e-mails usually have bullet points of key talking points along with a list of agreed-upon action steps and the people responsible for each of these items.

- Quite often, I find myself scheduling my next steps for follow up during a meeting. I find that scheduling follow-up e-mails and phone calls is extremely helpful in keeping things on track. I know that people are very busy and are prone to forget, so I try to help them with reminders without being a pest.

- I also try to schedule the next meeting or phone call before leaving the conversation. I find that this continues to create rhythm in the working relationship. There's nothing like going back and forth for weeks to find a mutually agreed-upon date. Save yourself the trouble and go into a meeting with a good grasp of when you might be available next.

- In a large project scenario, I use project management software to help guide the project for everyone involved. The time it takes to input expectations, roles, and responsibilities is well worth the return.

I know that many driven by a relational posture may think this approach is mechanical and artificial. Nevertheless, the potential awkwardness of creating a mutual agreement is far preferable to the level of frustration that often arises when this is not considered.

There's no doubt that collaboration is both powerful and necessary in our world. How to go about co-laboring is something we all need to help each other with. What works for you? Have you ever written down how you collaborate? It may be worth your time to think through some of this before your next opportunity to collaborate arises.

Good Idea (key thoughts from this section)	Now What? (your ideas and next steps for execution)
People are unpredictable, which makes collaboration complicated.	_____ _____ _____
Clearly state the kind of collaboration you think you are entering upfront, at the beginning of the relationship. Getting things down on paper, even if it's a simple one-sheet agreement, can make a world of difference.	_____ _____ _____
No matter how egalitarian an endeavor may *want* to be, it will still need people to take leadership in specific areas in order for the overall goal to become reality.	_____ _____

I Need It!

Time.
> Money.
> Fear.
Uncertainty.
Ego.

There are a million reasons why one might not collaborate with another. The reasons listed here, along with many more like them, are all legitimate and warrant consideration before entering into a collaborative relationship.

But first, more foundationally, I think you should consider how you view collaboration and what value you truly place on it. This will determine how much effort you are willing to put into working with others. The way you value collaboration probably falls into one of the following four categories:

1. **Collaboration as Optional:** Some view collaboration as a nice option for enhancing one's own endeavor. In this view, collaboration is something you add to your work when it's convenient and readily available. In this view, collaboration is not essential or actively sought. Those with this perspective believe that they are self-sufficient enough to accomplish their goals.

2. **Collaboration as Connecting:** Some view collaboration as simply connecting with others. It doesn't entail too much work outside of getting together. In this view, collaboration is mostly an intellectually satisfying experience with minimal commitment and

little expectation for specific outcomes. Things like relational or professional benefits are nice by-products of collaboration, but not the goal.

3. **Collaboration as Want:** Many view collaboration as something they want. They know it's extremely beneficial to moving their endeavors forward but find themselves perplexed by how collaboration actually works. Based on my interaction with leaders, I think most are in this category of thought. They genuinely want to collaborate but feel a sense of pessimism due to previous experiences and lack the energy to seriously try again.

4. **Collaboration as Necessity:** Only a small minority hold the view that collaboration is an absolute necessity in their pursuits. Despite some of the disappointments of past experiences, people who hold this perspective choose to open themselves up to new opportunities, even at the risk of being let down again. These individuals choose to learn from their past failures to become better collaborators and work intentionally toward paradigms, systems, and arrangements that produce great partnerships.

An Organization Created in Collaboration

In the spring of 2003, three young filmmakers from San Diego traveled to Uganda in search of a story. They had no idea that their trip would forever change the trajectory of their respective futures. Jason Russell, Bobby Bailey, and Laren Poole discovered the tragic realities of Africa's longest-running war and its impact on children. The conflict between the Lord's Resistance Army (LRA) and the Government of Uganda (GoU) include the forced recruitment of young children to fight the war. As a result, 1.8 million children were displaced from their homes as they fled for their lives.

Upon seeing this firsthand, these three filmmakers returned home and created a documentary that exposed this ongoing injustice in Uganda. As storytellers, they knew that the story had to be shared with as many people as possible to create the kind of global awareness that would ultimately lead to international intervention. They started a nonprofit organization called Invisible Children, a fitting description for the millions that have been displaced and forgotten.

Using the power of media, Invisible Children has collaborated and mobilized millions toward ending this conflict in Africa. They have committed themselves to long-term development, working directly with a Ugandan staff, to provide much-needed help, including the building of schools, clean water and sanitation, technology and power, and savings and loans initiatives. Through it all, they have kept the collaborative spirit upon which the organization was founded.

Ben Keesey is now the executive director and chief executive officer (CEO) of Invisible Children. He also happens to be a good friend. In the midst of all his recent travels, Ben took some time to speak with me about their organization's collaborative process as well as lessons they've learned over the years about collaborating with other groups.

Invisible Children has strategically structured its organization to allow ideas to flow down from the top as well as bubble up from the staff who work under the supervision of managers. The three original founders form The Executive Council and meet quarterly to develop ideas to present to their management team, which consists of 12 managers. Invisible Children's management team tries to gather every six months to facilitate vision-casting conversations. All ideas, whether produced by the three founders or from anyone else in the organization, are tested against the opinions of the 12 managers. As Ben says, "For one of our ideas or campaigns to truly succeed, all aspects of our company have to be behind it. Everyone has to be on board and fulfill his or her role. We need full consensus in order to move forward." It is the mission of the management team to challenge, critique, reject, or shape the ideas that are presented while keeping the overall mission in mind.

Ben shared that they regularly create *listening space* that allows everyone working for Invisible Children to submit ideas and thoughts about the organization. These moments are treasured and intentionally created to build a culture of collaboration.

In regard to working with other groups, Ben chuckled at some of their earlier mistakes in collaborating with anyone and everyone—just for asking. The only requirement in those days was that the collaborators have a heartbeat. Invisible Children has learned over the years that collaboration will work only when there's a good fit—both of heart and of goals—between the parties involved. As a result, they have instituted a more thorough vetting process for new collaborative opportunities.

I love organizations like Invisible Children that remain open to collaboration in order to produce greater impact. If you view collaboration as a necessity, a world of new opportunities will open up to you and you will experience perspectives that otherwise might never have been possible.

Good Idea (key thoughts from this section)	Now What? (your ideas and next steps for execution)
How you view collaboration and the value you place on it will determine how much intentional effort you are willing to put into working with others.	_____
Many leaders genuinely want to collaborate but feel a sense of pessimism due to previous experiences and lack the energy to seriously try again.	_____
Collaboration will work only when there's a good fit—both of heart and of goals—between the parties involved.	_____

CHAPTER

34

Do You Trust Me?

"**Y**ou're not listening."

"Yes, I am."

"What did I just say?"

"Yeah, I know. You were talking about that thing. You know, the thing . . ."

(Frustrated stare.)

("Caught in the act" stare back.)

"Never mind."

"Come on."

Heard that before? It's the all-too-familiar conversation that takes place between younger couples trying to figure out how to partner together in life. But that same conversation could just as easily be two people seeking a professional partnership. It may not come out in these exact words, but the core problem of not listening well can often become a source of great strife that may eventually lead to a parting of ways. Our failure to listen clearly communicates our uninterest in and lack of focus on the things that the other party believes are important. Trust often hinges upon whether the other person senses our sincere interest in the collaborative endeavor.

Keep in mind that hearing someone physically is a far cry from actually listening to him or her. Listening well is both an art form to develop and a skill to refine. It is an area we must all regularly work on.

Our mind has the ability to take in or block out information based on our sense of its importance. It's all about priorities and values. Unfortunately, the chaos of your life can drown out important connection opportunities

147

with people we really do need to listen to. How many partnerships have been lost because of our inability to listen well? How many opportunities have passed us by because we could not hear anyone outside of our own ego?

I recently overheard a very loud conversation at a coffee shop between the owner of a creative agency and a disgruntled client. The client communicated how frustrated he was at the owner's inability to listen to his requests. He went through a list of four to five key items that he had communicated by both e-mail and phone. The woman who owned the agency looked flustered. Initially, she was very defensive and tried to correct the client. Unfortunately for her, he was well prepared with documents that supported his claims. Toward the end of the conversation, she finally admitted that she had been working off of assumptions and had not taken the time to seriously consider his requests.

Ouch. The failure to listen can put quite a crimp in any business's success and growth.

Although I am the last one to claim expertise in this area (just ask my wife), I've learned and incorporated a few things into my life that have made me a better listener. The following little tweaks that I've made along the way have made a world of difference in my ability to collaborate effectively with others:

- **Pay attention to names.** Okay, I know what many of you are thinking: "I'm just not good at remembering names."

  I get it. It's impossible to remember all the names of the people we meet. Right?

  The problem is not so much that we have an inability to remember every person we meet. Rather, I think the problem is that some of us have given up on the notion of even *trying* to remember the names of others. I used to embrace this kind of thinking. Finally, after several embarrassing "What's your name again?" conversations, I decided to develop a strategy for remembering names.

  Here are some things that I do that help me recall the names of people I meet:

  o **Repetition:** I try to use the name of the person I've just met several times during that initial conversation. I have found that this repetition dramatically increases my ability to remember that person's name later.

o **Writing It Down:** I will often enter the person's name, along with some key words that will remind me of the conversation, directly into my phone—even while we are still meeting. Be sure to tell the person that you're speaking with what you are doing so that they don't think you're texting someone else.

o **Replay:** I've found that sharing with someone else a brief synopsis of a conversation I've just had really helps solidify the details of the conversation in my mind—including the names of the people involved. You can't do this all the time, but when possible, it's a good exercise that works.

- **Stay present.** Don't be *that guy* who scans the room during a conversation for bigger fish to move on to. Not only does this suck for the person speaking with you, but you will miss out on the opportunity at hand. You know what I'm talking about. The whole "I'm too cool for this conversation, so I'll look for someone else" attitude will ultimately backfire on you. And when it does, you'll deserve it! (I'm just saying.)

  Don't engage people if you're not going to be present both physically and mentally. Keep in mind that our bodies communicate as much as our mouths. If you're not interested, excuse yourself and walk away. Don't act like you're interested and waste people's time. Being present also requires eye contact. I think this is a common courtesy that everyone deserves. Train yourself to maintain eye contact and remain present during your conversations. The rewards are worth the effort.

- **Ask clarifying questions.** I think one of the best ways to engage others is through great questions that clarify what the person is trying to communicate. This is especially important in conversations about collaboration. Asking questions such as, "Would you mind clarifying what you mean by that?" or "Would you give me an example of what you're referring to?" will help crystallize the other person's intent and expectations. Asking clarifying questions also communicates your deep level of interest in the person and in the efforts you're hoping to embark on together. This can help build strong credibility and trust in the relationship.

- **Listen to the why and not just the what.** People don't usually say all of what they really mean to say or want to say; generally, a lot is held back in conversation. On the other hand, some of the things said in frustration or pain are rarely as bad as they initially sound. You have to listen for what the person's heart is trying to communicate—not just the words used. Try to assess the context of the conversation and put yourself in the shoes of the one communicating.

I'm reminded of what Indian philosopher Jiddu Krishnamurti once said: "So when you are listening to somebody, completely, attentively, then you are listening not only to the words, but also to the feeling of what is being conveyed, to the whole of it, not part of it."

- **Take good notes.** When appropriate, take notes when talking to others. This will keep you engaged and focused on the conversation. Taking notes uses additional senses, which will help you better absorb and process what's *really* being said. In meetings, don't just rely on one assigned notetaker to do all the work. Throw that model of engagement away! It's highly unlikely that you're going to do anything with someone else's notes anyway. Don't relieve yourself of the responsibility of taking notes; it is an opportunity to be more engaged in developing a collaborative relationship.

- **Don't talk too much.** I know it sounds self-evident, but don't take over the conversation if your goal is to listen better. As far as I can tell, talking prevents you from listening well.

Consider what Oliver Wendell Holmes once said:

It is the province of knowledge to speak, and it is the province of wisdom to listen.

Listening well is an important part of collaboration and takes intentional effort to develop. If done well, it will open up a new world of relationships and opportunities.

Can you hear me now?

Good Idea (key thoughts from this section)	Now What? (your ideas and next steps for execution)
The failure to listen can damage a business's potential success and growth.	

Good Idea (key thoughts from this section)	Now What? (your ideas and next steps for execution)
Trust in collaboration often hinges upon whether the other person senses our sincere interest in the collaborative endeavor.	_____ _____ _____
"It is the province of knowledge to speak, and it is the province of wisdom to listen."	_____ _____ _____

Fight Club

1st RULE: You do not talk about FIGHT CLUB.
2nd RULE: You DO NOT talk about FIGHT CLUB.
3rd RULE: If someone says "stop," goes limp, or taps out, the fight is over.
4th RULE: Only two guys to a fight.
5th RULE: One fight at a time.
6th RULE: No shirts, no shoes.
7th RULE: Fights will go on as long as they have to.
8th RULE: If this is your first night at FIGHT CLUB, you HAVE to fight.
Welcome to FIGHT CLUB!

There's a big, fat elephant in the room.
It's called TENSION.
One of the truths about teamwork or collaboration is that it will produce tension in the work environment. I have yet to see a strong team of leaders or innovators work without some level of tension. In fact, companies and organizations that produce great quality often get there by facilitating a healthy fight culture.

Some of you already recognize the rules listed above from the movie *Fight Club*, a film about an underground fighting club created by an unnamed, discontented white-collared automobile company employee played by Edward Norton. It was an adaption of a 1996 novel by Chuck Palahniuk that creatively communicates the despair and paralysis that many people feel living in a system they have not created and living the kind of life they never wanted to live. The fighting in the film was about the attempt of everyman to *feel* again in a society that had made him numb.

I'm not saying we should just throw down with others at work (although I see that thought being attractive to some of you). But I do wonder if we've created a culture that overly values consensus and equality when it comes to ideas. In my opinion, all ideas are *not* created equally. There is a big difference between respectfully allowing everyone to have input (without contention) and collectively refining an idea in order to implement it well (and fighting it out when we disagree).

Tension is a good thing. In fact, it's quite necessary for teamwork.

Unfortunately, some teams settle for an agree-to-disagree escape clause that actually causes paralysis in organizational development. Although this neutral approach may work on some conversational level, it won't help move things forward. Decisions must be made. Addressing tension head-on (with some tact, of course) will birth much-needed clarity and productivity.

The following is a list of thoughts that may guide you toward developing a healthy fight culture in your collaborative efforts:

- **Invite people to fight.** Creating a culture that allows for healthy tension requires us to be open about what we hope to achieve. Be upfront. Invite the people you're working with to disagree and question. Be sure to communicate that the goal is to move the work forward. Therefore, the fight shouldn't revolve around personal attacks. Although it's difficult for most to separate work from personal criticism, reemphasizing the need for healthy tension goes a long way.

- **Determine some basic fight club rules.** Most people look for some kind of guidelines for engagement. What's allowed? What's out of bounds? Are there opportunities during meetings for feedback, suggestions, and/or pushback when needed? Who ultimately decides? Do people understand this?

- **Play by the rules and model the fight.** There's nothing more disappointing than seeing a leader who first hypes up collaboration and then ignores the input of others. In these cases, the leader was at best ignorant about what true collaboration involves or at worst disingenuous with his or her words. Those who want to benefit from healthy tension must model it well and play by the rules. If you're going to welcome a fight, you have to be open to the thoughts of others and provide your team with plenty of examples of listening, refining concepts based on their feedback, and responding nondefensively. People are not going to trust that you believe in the value of collaborative tension until they see you living it out.

- **Keep the fight underground.** If the goal of working through tension is about moving the core mission of the organization forward, then it's imperative to determine who speaks about it as well as who needs to know about it. In most scenarios, agreeing to work through the details internally in confidentiality is probably smart. This may sound like common sense to you, but I've seen groups share information that the public didn't need to know—and may not have even been interested in hearing! Unless you're developing the next iPhone, you might be surprised to learn how little the public is interested in your internal affairs.

  The only real exception to this kind of confidentiality is if you are seeking public feedback on possible idea direction. In this case, be prepared to communicate clearly and often as to the purpose and goals for public input. Also, develop a process for receiving and analyzing data as well as reporting back to the public once completed. Taking things public often requires public accountability.

- **Celebrate the win together.** The win is in the team moving forward with an idea. Celebrate well when a team comes together and works through its differences. Although the solution may not feel ideal for everyone involved, it will almost always be better than remaining at a standstill. Party well when significant progress is made. Be sure to publicly recognize team members and reward them when possible. This builds team morale, momentum, and confidence for working together in the future.

  Although the thoughts listed here aren't perfect, they can provide some parameters for productively engaging team tension. And remember that this entire process depends on complex human beings, the ultimate variable. In addition, tension over an idea is one thing, but interpersonal conflict that arises among team members can be exponentially more difficult to navigate.

It's never easy, but it's an essential part of leadership. The growth and health of an organization often depends on leadership's ability to engage in difficult conversations during times of tension or conflict. Avoiding or ignoring these opportunities (yes, opportunities) for maturity has led to the unnecessary demise of many endeavors. Here are some insights/lessons I've learned over the years in dealing with conflict that I hope you find helpful:

- **Meet in person.** When possible, choose the more uncomfortable and inconvenient option of meeting in person. Other forms of communication such as e-mail, text messages, social media replies, and phone calls rarely capture our intent or produce healthy results. Also, meeting in person puts flesh on the conflict. In other words, we can't hide behind technology (and our insecurities) when we're face to face with another human being.

  I know that most people don't enjoy or thrive in confrontational situations, but I have yet to find a more productive way to engage someone at his or her core being than face to face. Initiate this conversation whenever possible. Unless the person you're in conflict with is completely dense, he or she should see the value in meeting in person. If the person is dense, good luck.

- **Listen well.** As discussed in Chapter 34, listening well is essential to building a relationship. And remember, there's a difference between listening well and just waiting for an opportunity to throw out your next argument. No matter how difficult it is in the heat of the moment, try to listen for what the person is really trying to say. Consider the underlying presuppositions and try to identify what led the person to think as he or she currently does. Is the person being reasonable? Could the person actually be accurate in some views, especially given his or her scope of experience?

  After hearing the person out, take time to rearticulate the person's frustration by saying it back to him or her. This provides evidence that you (1) were listening and (2) understand why the person is frustrated or angry to begin with. For many, this is the moment in the conversation when they will begin to see that you get it. To do this well, you really can't be defensive or distracted by other thoughts. Your goal is to listen. That's it!

- **Be clear.** The goal of a conflict resolution engagement is not to be right. Rather, the conversation should move both parties involved toward a greater understanding of the cause of the conflict as well as next steps toward its resolution. More often than not, it's misunderstanding that fuels a point of tension. Ask questions that could help clarify the situation. If the goal isn't to win the argument, these moments take on a totally different tenor—one that everyone involved will find refreshing.

- **Stay honest.** No one's perfect. It is quite possible that each person involved in the conflict has a skewed perspective of the situation. Be upfront and openly recognize that. Work toward the truth (if possible) and don't hide behind your ego and insecurity. The goal should be to learn and grow from the tension in order to move forward in a healthy way as a company, organization, or individual. Honesty is still the best policy. Most people are willing to forgive those who are honest and show genuine remorse for their actions.

- **Think action.** As you work through the conflict, take notes (both mentally and literally) on what can be done to curb future repeats. Share some of these thoughts with the other person(s) involved. Taking the posture of a learner is healthy and will benefit many more people along the way. Furthermore, stay true to your word and be sure to follow up on your commitment to change.

- **Have a neutral party there.** In some situations, it might be wise to have a neutral party there to witness and even moderate the conversation. This person is not there to be a judge, but rather a person who can steer the conversation toward a solution as well as provide accountability for all that's been said. Make sure that everyone involved is comfortable with the person who is chosen to moderate.

Tension, both at a personal and team level, can become a great catalyst for growth if we choose to approach it with humility and wisdom. Admittedly, working toward creating a team culture that is deeply committed to walking down the path of tension for the good of the company or organization is no easy task. It takes time and patience to develop. Nevertheless, it will be well worth it in the long run. Plus, it will make you a better human being—and that's always a good thing!

Good Idea (key thoughts from this section)	Now What? (your ideas and next steps for execution)
Organizations that produce great quality often get there by facilitating a healthy fight culture.	
There is a big difference between respectfully allowing everyone to have input (without contention) and collectively refining an idea in order to implement it well (and fighting it out when we disagree).	
People are not going to trust that you believe in the value of collaborative tension until they see you living it out.	
Celebrate well when a team comes together and works through its differences. Although the solution may not feel ideal for everyone involved, it will almost always be better than remaining at a standstill.	

CHAPTER

36

The Hire

I am convinced that nothing we do is more important than hiring and developing people. At the end of the day you bet on people, not on strategies.
—Larry Bossidy, former chief executive officer
(CEO) of Honeywell

I t's all about people, isn't it?

It's about working with the right people at the right time for the right purpose. Ultimately, *people* drive vision, embody values, and grow the influence of a company or organization. No people, no organization. Wrong people, wrong organization.

As your company or organization continues to grow, it becomes essential to develop a strategy for hiring well. Adding the right people to your work, whether internally or externally, can be the difference between business as usual and exponential impact. The sustainability and scalability of an idea is often contingent upon whom, when, why, and how you hire.

Hiring is so much more than simply adding an employee or a partner to an endeavor. It is an invitation to collaborate and shape the future of something deemed valuable and significant.

Here are some principles that can help guide the hiring process:

- **Determine whether the hire is essential right now.** Before you take steps toward hiring, be sure to do the due diligence of assessing the actual needs of your company or organization. I'm not talking about an anecdotal assessment that's based on a few "I think we need" conversations or suggestions from people. There should be real data that support the decision to look for someone to hire. This will require you to review your fiscal numbers, determine the current trajectory of your activity and growth, and consider the impact of new hires on your team dynamics and productivity.

Time is money—so is timing. Many believe that the right time to hire is when you *absolutely need* someone to fulfill a specified role in order for the company or organization to accomplish its mission. I agree. The ideal time to hire is when the efficiency and effectiveness of work is seriously stifled by the absence of a specific role. Until then, the team should look for alternative options to sustain and grow the endeavor by picking up extra responsibilities or outsourcing work. This is usually more cost effective in the short run and provides a window to save up for hiring that new person when he or she is absolutely needed.

- **Develop objectives for the hire.** Hiring, like most other things in business, should be driven by clear objectives. Don't limit these objectives to just the responsibilities of the position. They should also encompass how you see the person or role adding value to the company's future. Remember, you are not just hiring someone to do the job. You want people to take their functions to a whole new level and become positive influences and models for the rest of the team. Always be mindful that you are adding someone who will help shape the future of your company, whether at a micro or macro level. Choose wisely, communicate clearly, and determine ahead of time what you hope to accomplish in the overall picture.

- **Create a slow hiring process and think company investment.** By nature, most hiring opportunities feel urgent. Nevertheless, resist the urge to hire on a whim or in reaction to an immediate need. You might get lucky, but generally, this is not a good move. Typically, you'll pay dearly for abrupt and spontaneous hiring.

  Take it slow whenever possible. Think in terms of months, not weeks. This is why most good companies require multiple interviews with several interdepartment leaders for a potential hire. It's not so much about making people jump through hoops. Rather, it's a system that allows for a holistic vetting process that seeks the greatest good for the company as well as for the person being interviewed. Hiring well takes time.

Keep in mind as well that most new hires require quite a bit of time and resource investment for integration into their role. I once heard Frank Markow, an organizational leadership consultant, speak about the four kinds of people who join a team:

1. Those who are able and willing
2. Those who are unable, but willing
3. Those who are able, but unwilling
4. Those who are unable and unwilling

Based on these categorizations, you probably want to hire person 1 and avoid person 4. Unfortunately, when you are rushing to hire, you may not have this option. Thinking through hiring person 2 or person 3 will help you weigh what will be required from your company or organization to bring your new hire on board. For example, person 2 will require a lot of training time, whereas person 3 will require motivating incentives for involvement. Regardless, knowing what kind of person you're hiring will then give you a picture of what investment may be required to enable that person to fully contribute to the team.

- **Do your homework and ask good questions.** When the time comes to conduct an interview, you should be prepared and ready to go. In addition to reviewing an application and following up on references, some recommend that you do an online search about the person seeking the position. I'll leave that decision up to you. The point here is that you need to know everything you can about any individual whom you're thinking about adding to your team.

   During the interview, don't be shy. Ask thought-provoking questions. As long as you aren't being a jerk about it, most people will be intrigued and engaged by this approach. For example, instead of asking what was most challenging in their previous job, why not ask to see if they have any sense of what might be most challenging in the position they are applying for? This kind of open-ended questioning lends itself to more creative and insightful responses. Beyond qualifications on paper and expected answers to standard questions, try to look for qualities of initiative and critical thinking. Remember, you're looking for linchpins, not those who will simply conform to company politics.

- **Look for cultural fit.** As you interview people for a new role, always ask yourself if the person is a good cultural fit. You and your team will have to work with this person daily and in close proximity.

You may spend more time with this new hire than you do with your own family! It's imperative that you get a clear sense of how you see this person fitting in. I usually look for some feedback from team members as well as trusted friends and mentors whom I consider to be knowledgeable in the area of hiring. Finally, do you even *like* the candidate? Don't discount this important criterion. You want to hire only people who will enhance and further reinforce the culture you are trying to create in your organization.

- **Embrace the opportunity.** Potential hires can give you some great insights and advice on the future of your company. If they have done their homework, they should be able to provide some great outside thoughts about your work. Why not take the opportunity to explore how you could make your company better? The great thing about human interaction, even in a hiring scenario, is that you could walk away from it with a great new relationship—and perhaps some new perspectives and ideas for your life and work.

Executing your ideas requires working with a great team—whether internal or external. Take the time to assemble the right people around you.

Good Idea (key thoughts from this section)	Now What? (your ideas and next steps for execution)
Ultimately, *people* drive vision, embody values, and grow the influence of a company or organization.	
Adding the right people to your work, whether internally or externally, can be the difference between business as usual and exponential impact.	
As you interview, always ask yourself if the person is a good cultural fit—and if you even *like* him or her.	

Taking It Further

- Consider the last project you collaborated on. Was it a positive experience? If so, what do you attribute it to? If not, what went wrong?
- Think of someone you'd like to collaborate with on a current idea you are trying to execute. Write a simple one-page agreement that includes a few metrics for success.
- How much do you value collaboration? How essential is it to your work? Which of the four categories in Chapter 33 is most reflective of the way you have viewed collaboration?
- Have you ever lost a partnership or relationship because you weren't listening well? Ever miss out on an opportunity because you couldn't hear anyone outside of your own ego? What could you have done differently that might have led to a different outcome? (See the list in Chapter 34 for some hints.)
- Does your organization have rules for fighting? What's allowed? What's out of bounds? If you don't have rules for fighting, write some basic ones now that you would like to see used to encourage and guide healthy conflict.
- Can you think of a time when you or your boss made a poor hiring decision? Looking back from your perspective today, what was the reason for the bad decision?

Getting Out There!

Why Brand Matters

A pple
Target
Starbucks
Coca-Cola
Disney
Google
Amazon

These iconic brands are shaping our global culture. Not only are they driving and shaping our consumptive behaviors, they also are strategically refining the way we interact as human beings and how we think about the world. Brands matter in ways that go far deeper than a purchase or donation decision. They're guiding our present and creating our future.

Whether you acknowledge it or not, your product, company, or cause has a brand. You have a brand. Your brand is embedded in everything that you communicate, facilitate, and produce. Your brand highlights the distinctiveness with which you embody your mission.

And if you want to execute your idea well, you need to know the answer to this question: What kind of brand do you have?

To strategically develop a brand, it may be beneficial to clarify two things that a brand is *not:*

1. **Your brand is not your mission.**

   In most companies and organizations, leaders will spend a significant amount of time (and rightly so) on the development and refinement of its mission, vision, and values. This focus provides the foundation for any endeavor. The problem arises when leadership takes a new discovery and immediately moves to marketing a message across multiple platforms (e.g., websites, newsletters, programs, social media, and design) while bypassing the development of their brand.

   This usually results in brand confusion, unrealistic perceptions, and expectations (both inside and outside of the organization) and systematic inconsistency that will ultimately hinder development and growth. Although your mission identifies why you exist, your brand embodies your organizational personality, identity, and voice.

   For example, Nike's slogan, "Just do it," doesn't necessarily communicate the company's mission to help athletes reach their human potential through its innovative products. Rather, the tagline captures an emotion and encapsulates an attitude—the kind of attitude with which it hopes to inspire all the athletes who use its products.

   You see, it's quite possible for the leadership of a company or organization to collectively agree on a common mission and set of values but have totally different expectations for what the brand should be like. For example, a board may agree to the organizational value of creativity but hold varying expectations of how creativity will be expressed. Some may be thinking of Apple while others are thinking more of Van Gogh—two very different perspectives when it comes to how creativity is expressed by a brand.

   Creatives often have a hard time obtaining approval from governing bodies when they are producing work that expresses a brand's identity. Usually this is because they haven't sought a clear understanding of the brand strategy. Instead, they allow the conversation to be driven by their personal creative preferences.

   If you want your idea to be accepted and executed, know your brand strategy.

2. **Your brand is not just a cool design or tagline.**

   Your brand is much more than a good design or a well-crafted message. It's really about understanding your personality and voice and then creating memorable brand experiences—at every point of contact with the brand—that your constituents will identify with and find remarkable. A strong and sustainable branding of an idea will translate your identity and effectively communicate it across multiple, audience-specific platforms and campaigns. A successful brand develops relational trust over time that results in deep loyalty.

Your brand encompasses the kinds of attributes you would want people to think about whenever they consider you and your work. Think of your brand as an internal filter through which you determine how you want to be known in the public eye. Your brand will ultimately affect your language, aesthetics, design, online presence, staffing, and infrastructure.

A Practical Guide to Branding

Here are some practical thoughts that may help you get started (or restarted) on developing a strong brand:

- **Engage (or reengage) your brand.** Spend some time writing down your perceptions of your organization's brand attributes. Try coming up with 10 to 15 adjectives that describe your brand. Be honest and write the first things that come to mind. Don't overanalyze! Once you've done it, invite fellow team members to participate in this exercise as well. Be sure to share your thoughts with one another and see if you are all on the same page. You may also want to get open-ended input from your end users, customers, and/or supporters. Try to use questions that use metaphors to draw out opinion. Here are some samples:
  - o If our company were a clothing store, what kind of clothing store would we be and why? What if we were a restaurant?
  - o If our company were a friend, what kinds of events would you be comfortable inviting us to? A holiday party? A Superbowl party? A black-tie event? A weekend getaway?
- **Identify your main brand attributes** (usually three to five) and review them regularly with your leadership. Conduct creative learning experiences that will reinforce your brand in the same way you reinforce your mission. Your leaders are the key influencers of your brand, so it is vital for them to be included in the process.

- **Check for consistency** in communication of your brand across multiple platforms. Do you sound and feel like the same company on your website as you do on Facebook or Twitter? How about in your newsletters and your e-mails? What does your workspace communicate?
- **If budget allows, consider bringing in an outside voice** that has experience in organizational brand development. View it as an investment toward future clarity. Good branding will save you time and money in the long run.

A strong brand will move people to action and create deep loyalty. A weak brand will often prevent people from understanding or even seeing the mission and vision of a company or organization. Developing a brand takes time but is essential to the success of any endeavor hoping to reach its full potential.

Good Idea (key thoughts from this section)	Now What? (your ideas and next steps for execution)
Your brand is embedded in everything that you communicate, facilitate, and produce.	_____ _____ _____
Your leaders are the key influencers of your brand, so it is vital for them to be included in the process.	_____ _____ _____
Your brand can move people to action and create deep loyalty. It takes time to develop a strong brand but is essential to the success of any endeavor hoping to reach its full potential.	_____ _____ _____

CHAPTER
38

A Personal Brand?

I recently asked Jonathan, my eight-year-old son, "What do you think Daddy does for work?"

He answered, "Dad, you help people with their ideas."

I replied, "That's amazing! Can I hire you?"

We both giggled.

Despite our limited conversations about my consulting work, my son had picked up the fact that I was passionate about helping people with their ideas and was able to brand me accordingly. To Jonathan, I am a dad, a husband, and a guy who helps others with ideas. He got it. Maybe I will hire him.

The idea of developing a strong personal brand is definitely coming up more often in my conversations with clients and friends. People want to know how to develop and leverage their personal brand. They recognize that a personal brand can really be a benefit if used wisely.

Simply put, a personal brand is a reference to the public perception of an individual's identity. It includes how people perceive our personality and our associations with specific ideas, products, companies, organizations, and so on.

Like it or not, people have already branded you. This means that when people think of you, they think of specific attributes. Maybe you're the friendly, considerate, and resourceful friend everyone turns to. Maybe you're the creative innovator that people call on when they need ideas for a new product. Maybe you're the authority who comes to mind when people think of board games. Whatever it is, you've been branded. It's possible that whenever specific words or ideas come up in conversation, people bring you up because they feel you embody a particular idea.

171

So, how do you develop your personal brand?

Here's my paradoxical answer: You can't, but you can.

Here's what I mean . . .

A personal brand is developed when there is more than one person involved. The concept of a brand implies that there is one person communicating the brand and another perceiving it. This means that developing your personal brand requires more than just you.

So what's the secret to creating your personal brand? It's simple: stop working on it! I recommend that you change your focus from working on your brand to working on your work. Strong brands are created and sustained because of the consistent quality of the work that is produced. In a day and age of user reviews, blogs, and social media, a brand that does not produce quality work will simply not survive.

Too many people spend far too much time and energy thinking about their brand without focusing enough on what they're actually hoping to create—the work itself. Take away the quality of work or the quality of your character and you will have a weak brand. At best, you will possess only hype.

Here's the equation to use when developing a personal brand:

$$\text{Quality of work} \times \text{Integrity} = \text{Personal brand}$$

Some may produce great work, but if they lack character, it's highly unlikely that they will produce a strong personal brand. Any number times zero always equals zero. In the same way, if someone of great character doesn't produce good-quality work, that person too is unlikely to develop a strong brand.

Want a strong personal brand? Keep producing quality that people will appreciate and tell others about. Is what you're creating something that is worth talking about? In addition, be a person of integrity who models authenticity, reliability, and a commitment to deliver what has been promised. Resist the urge to simply mass market yourself. If you do, you'll just come across as just that—a self-consumed mass marketer. And you know how we all love those folks. You don't have to platform yourself in this manner to build your brand.

Personal branding is paradoxical. Since it involves other people, there will always be elements you can't control. Focus on what you can control—the quality of your work—and allow others to develop your brand by sharing the stories of their experiences with you and your work.

There's nothing inherently wrong with wanting to be known for something you're passionate about. Just keep in mind that a strong personal brand is a great by-product of our pursuit for quality and integrity, but a horrible goal for our work.

Accidental Lessons about Personal Branding

People say hindsight is 20/20. I suppose this is somewhat true.

When I consider how I've developed my own personal brand as an idea guy, I must admit that I had no such intentions when I started out. I've always loved ideas and knew early on that ideas could and have indeed changed the world throughout history. The thought of exploring how our ideas work has been a longtime fascination of mine. This led me to pursue graduate studies in philosophy. My hope was that schooling would help me become a better thinker. The program kicked my butt—and my gut—multiple times. It was a daily challenge to do the work, but I stuck with it.

Over time, people started to give me opportunities to speak about the creative process and help solve problems within their organizations. I soon found myself working with not-for-profits, city-based initiatives, and faith communities. Soon, companies began approaching me for help with their ideas, given my track record in the nonprofit space, especially in the area of building creative campaigns. Most of the ideas I had worked on revolved around creating more social good in our world, and little did I know that cause-marketing and corporate social responsibility (CSR) would become such hot topics in the corporate world. Before I knew it, I was regularly associated with concepts such as creativity, innovation, social good, and leadership.

During this time, I started a blog so that I could capture some of my thoughts on these various topics. I never expected anyone to actually read it! To my surprise, people started to engage, follow, and push me into new areas of thought. I also started to dabble in the emerging world of social media and sought ways to leverage its network potential toward creating social good. I worked to learn all I could and hoped for the best. Whether it was viral initiatives, flash mobs, or conferences I created, everything seemed to work out much better than expected and led to new opportunities.

I worked hard on being consistent, open to diverse thinking, and collaborative in my approach. I knew that relationships would be important in whichever area I decided to pursue. I went out of my way to build friendships, platform the ideas of others, and help people network and connect with one another. I was well aware that my hopes of creating meaningful ideas for our world would have to be much bigger than myself. I openly introduced people to one another and did a ton of free work on projects

I believed in. Looking back, although I was exhausted on many occasions, all of those pro bono opportunities really helped me sharpen my skills in the area of implementing ideas.

I still can't believe that I now make a living helping others develop and implement their ideas. My personal brand as an idea maker was really the result of wholeheartedly pursuing an area of passion. I didn't care whether I was ever going to get paid for my efforts. I knew that paying my dues early would eventually pay off. I invested regularly in people and projects that I believed in. I'm so glad I did. I think I'm a better human being because of this experience.

Was my personal brand developed intentionally? Yes and no. I hope that now you understand the paradox.

Good Idea (key thoughts from this section)	Now What? (your ideas and next steps for execution)
Simply put, a personal brand is a reference to the public perception of an individual's identity.	_____ _____ _____
Like it or not, people have already branded you.	_____ _____ _____
Change your focus from working on your brand to working on your work.	_____ _____ _____
Focus on what you can control— the quality of your work—and allow others to develop your brand by sharing the stories of their experiences with you and your work.	_____ _____ _____

The Pitch

In 1988, I took a huge step forward into adulthood. That was the year
I first fell in love. I had just turned 16, but I can still remember my first
passion vividly.

No, it wasn't a girl. It was a white 1978 Toyota Celica Coupe!

Now, before you look up this sweet ride online, I must remind you that
it was a cool car back then (at least in my mind). Granted, the car was 10
years old, but I didn't care. It was mine! When my parents gave it to me,
I felt great independence as well as a newfound trust from them.

I still remember walking into the car dealership where my uncle worked
as a salesman. No disrespect to my uncle, but he played the part of a
stereotypical car dealer to a tee. He had the slicked back hair, the nice
suit, and that little sparkle in his teeth. I love him, but at that moment,
I didn't know if I could trust him. I vividly remember him making the
sales pitch—going through all the details of why we should buy the used
Celica over all the other vehicles on the lot. I kept thinking, "Uncle, it's
us. We're your family. Why are you pitching so hard?" Still, with each new
feature he highlighted, my excitement increased. Fortunately for us, my
uncle wasn't out to rip us off. He was true to his word, and the car was just
as he promised. I can see now why he did so well in sales.

I learned something that day: pitching an idea takes passion, knowledge,
and an ability to deliver on the goods promised.

All idea makers will eventually have to pitch or sell their idea to someone else. Whether it's pitching to a potential investor, team member,
or customer, the pitch process can be one of the most exhilarating or

frightening experiences in life. You're being called upon to share something deeply personal that you've been working on.

As you think about how best to pitch your idea, consider some of the following lessons I've learned while pitching my own ideas as well as listening to others pitch theirs:

- **When possible, start by building relationship.**

  This may sound obvious, but too many people think they can just shortcut through relationship building and just get to the pitch. I receive e-mails on a consistent basis from people who want to be introduced to some of my more influential friends so that they can help accelerate their ideas. I honestly love making these connections, but they have to be rooted in relationship. Each introduction is a reflection of who I am. If someone I remotely know approaches me, I am going to be far more hesitant in connecting the person with my friends.

  Brad Lomenick is a person who gets pitched to all the time by people who want to put their products in front of the large network of his organization, Catalyst. "Build relational equity before you launch into something," Brad advises. "It may not always be possible, but when it is possible, it's always something good to do. It's not that we only consider friends, but it sure helps that they are in relationship with us."

  He continued, "Most great ideas seem to carry their weight in their source. We will often pursue an idea not because the pitch is good but because the person giving the idea is trusted and respected. The source makes a huge difference."

  Relationships matter in the pitching process. It will be well worth your time to develop relationships long before there's ever a need to pitch your idea. The general rule is that the higher up the ladder you go, the more relational equity will be necessary.

- **Keep it clear, short, and simple.**

  What is it that you're pitching? Can the core concept be communicated clearly in a few seconds? Will it pass the elevator pitch test?

  Imagine yourself standing in an elevator on your way down from the 30th floor when another person asks, "So, what's your idea about?" Will you be able to communicate succinctly and effectively enough to spark the person's interest or desire for further conversation?

  Clarity, brevity, and simplicity are essential to the pitch.

Be sure to work extra hard on this. There's nothing more distracting than listening to someone pitching an idea that he or she doesn't appear to have a clear understanding of! Your credibility—and the listener's interest—will quickly start to take a nosedive if you aren't ready for these pitch moments. Preparation is key, whether the pitch moment is spontaneous or planned.

Simplifying and clarifying a concept takes many hours of work. Even if you are a natural communicator, it doesn't necessarily mean your thoughts will make sense. Intelligent people who invest in ideas will see beyond a person's charm and identify whether there is any substance to the idea.

Be sure to write down the pitch and then spend time refining it. It also doesn't hurt to rehearse it in front of friends and family who are willing to provide feedback. You may also want to record your pitch on camera to see how it might be perceived by the one hearing it.

- **Don't forget the why.**

People who pitch well clearly communicate the why of their idea. In other words, these individuals don't focus solely on what they do or how they do it; they also share why they do it. The what of an idea usually points to features. The how of an idea often points to method. The why of an idea points to motive or reasons. This is where you will capture people emotionally, and people make decisions based on their emotions.

This is a marketing principle that is highly effective in pitches. For example, if you were pitching a new paper cup company, you could present the idea at three levels:

(i) The what: We produce high-quality cups.

(ii) The how: We produce high-quality paper cups using recycled materials.

(iii) The why: We produce high-quality paper cups using recycled materials because we deeply care about the environment and think that good business is possible without hurting the world we live in.

Each level of the pitch creates deeper levels of brand loyalty. As you pitch an idea, be sure to communicate not only what and how you do something but also why you are so passionate about the concept.

- **Think humble tenacity.**

   Do you believe in what you're pitching? Prove it!

   Prove it both with your words and your body language.

   Stay confident without being arrogant. Be honest without apologizing for a lack of knowledge. Remain tenacious without being overbearing.

   Scott Harrison of charity: water recently shared his thoughts with me about pitching an idea. Here's what he said:

   > Be truly passionate about your idea. People are infected by passion and turned off by the rote [action of] just going through the motions . . . . Tenacity is also really important—go out there and tell your story and be okay when people say no. If they say no, then just go on to the next person and the next person and the next person. It's grit. It's determination. You must choose not to be moved from the course of telling your story. Don't let the discouragement of initial rejection sap your passion.

   In other words, be confident in what you're pitching. If you believe in what you're doing, make sure people can sense it. If you can't communicate your own passion and confidence in the product, why would anyone get behind what you're doing?

   Worried about seeming arrogant? If you are worried about it, it's highly unlikely that you will be perceived as arrogant. It's the people who aren't aware of this or who don't care about it that come off as arrogant—usually because they are! Just in case, you can keep your confidence from turning into arrogance by rooting it in humility. Stay honest with the person you are pitching to. If you can't deliver the product or service at the scale the other party is asking for, say that. Be upfront and clearly communicate what you *can* do to help the person in his or her endeavor. Most will appreciate your honesty in the matter and seek viable ways to partner with you.

- **Do your homework.**

   Make sure you go into a meeting prepared to answer questions. Although you may not necessarily have all of the answers, you should have a firm grasp of the common issues surrounding your idea and know the questions that might arise. I've found that role-playing prior to a meeting is always helpful. You have to become the most aggressive critic of your own ideas.

In addition, do some homework on the person you're meeting with to understand why he or she might want to connect with your idea and partner with you. What makes this person someone you ought to meet and work with? What's in it for him or her? What needs will this partnership meet for that person? Take time to write these ideas down. Whenever possible, enter the meeting with data that support your reasoning. Keep in mind that you are there to show the other party how the partnership will benefit all sides. Ask yourself, "What is the potential return on investment for the person I am presenting to?"

- **Develop tangible pathways for involvement.**

Go into the meeting expecting a positive response. Why not?! If the idea is good and you've done your homework, then why shouldn't you expect a positive response? If this becomes the attitude with which you approach pitches, you should be ready for the next step—providing practical pathways for involvement when people do respond positively.

You must think beyond the pitch and be prepared with implementable action steps. Action steps will vary depending on the degree of interest and investment, so be sure to think through numerous ways a person could potentially get involved. Will you leave behind any materials? Will the other party need anything from you for further engagement? Does the person know whom to contact in the future? Put yourself in the other person's shoes and prepare accordingly. Don't let the opportunity slip through your fingers.

- **Make it remarkable.**

Seth Godin often describes *remarkable* as something that deserves a remark. Therefore, a remarkable experience causes the person experiencing it to tell others about it.

I think pitches ought to be remarkable. The reality is that most people we pitch our ideas to probably hear pitches regularly. How will you stand out? How will your pitch become memorable? Will your brochure packet break through the clutter? What is it about your pitch that would make the person share the idea with someone else?

Making a pitch remarkable requires some creativity. Think through how a person can experience your pitch with all five senses. It may sound silly, but I ask myself questions such as, "How will the other person taste my pitch? How will he or she touch my pitch? How will he or she smell my pitch?" This usually sparks some creative ways to communicate the idea.

The point here is that we should never settle for just communicating information in a one-dimensional way. When possible, work toward creating an overall experience that allows your idea to stay remarkable.

- **Follow up!**

Follow-up is critical. I can't make this point strongly enough! Whether it's an e-mail, personalized handwritten note, or a letter, always thank people for their time in a personal manner. Even if the person doesn't buy into your idea, keep the relationship open for future possibilities. Also, try to follow up within 24 hours of the meeting. This will help maintain momentum.

An Idea Worth Sharing

If your idea is something that the world needs, then there's no reason to be defensive, self-conscious, or insecure. Each pitch is an opportunity for someone else to participate in the growth of an idea designed to help everyone involved. If you believe in your idea, don't be shy when sharing it with others!

Good Idea (key thoughts from this section)	Now What? (your ideas and next steps for execution)
Pitching an idea takes passion, knowledge, and an ability to deliver on the goods promised.	_____
	_____
	_____
Too many people think they can just shortcut through relationship building and just get to the pitch.	_____
	_____
	_____

Good Idea (key thoughts from this section)	Now What? (your ideas and next steps for execution)
Keep your confidence from turning into arrogance by rooting it in humility.	_____ _____ _____
What is it about your pitch that would make the listener share your idea with someone else?	_____ _____ _____

Life in a Digital Age

Mad *Men* is a television show set in the glamorous world of 1960s Madison Avenue—advertising's mecca. It has won multiple awards for its historical authenticity and visual style. Although the show highlights some of the negative social issues of 1960s America, including sexism, racism, adultery, and homophobia, I enjoy watching it for its depiction of how marketing and advertising campaigns were shaped back in the day.

Until recent history, advertising agencies ruled our perception of products, services, and reality as a whole. They told us what to believe, like, and consume. And guess what? We drank the Kool-Aid they were dishing out. And then we asked for more.

My, how times have changed.

With the rise of the Internet and social media, we now have instant access to all kinds of valuable information—from price comparisons to peer reviews—that can help us make better purchase decisions. Companies now must listen to the public's feedback and suggestions for how to improve their products and services.

Meanwhile, ad agencies are scrambling to figure out what this shift means for marketing. Quite honestly, many have little idea of how to recalibrate for this new digital age. Smaller boutique agencies that are primarily focused on digital media are starting to win large accounts that were once held by the big well-known agencies.

The point?

Getting a new idea out there looks a whole lot different today than it once did. Although there are still foundational elements to good marketing, idea makers today must keep in mind that the landscape of sharing an idea with the public has changed. This doesn't mean that you just chuck all of the traditional marketing efforts out the door and embrace new media. Rather, it means you must take a holistic look at all of your options.

Aristotle had a lot to say about how to engage life's choices. He described virtue as a mean between two vices: (1) excess and (2) deficiency. For example, courage is a virtue that exists between two vices: (1) foolhardiness (or excess courage) that causes someone to blindly run into battle and (2) cowardice (or deficient courage) that prevents someone from even entering a battle.

The right choice often resides between two excesses. Although the choice of a marketing platform is not necessarily a moral one, I think Aristotle's approach can still be helpful. In my opinion, it's really not about whether you should choose traditional media over new media (or vice versa). I think there's wisdom somewhere in between. There's value to be found in both platforms.

For example, as much as some strongly lobby for moving solely to digital books, there will still be a market for people who want to carry a print book around and flip through the pages. Although some may still believe mailers are the way to go, others will view those companies as environmentally hostile and categorize them as spammers.

The following are some practical insights to sharing ideas in our digital world:

- **Move out of denial.**

   The world has changed. New media is not a fad. The train has left the station, and it's not coming back. Regardless of whether you decide to be active online on the various social media platforms, your customers are already there—and they are talking about you! The real question is, "Do you want to be part of the conversation?"

   Commit to developing an online strategy that works for your company or organization. It's okay to admit that you don't know what to do. The truth is that most people don't know what to do. But not knowing what to do is a poor excuse for not doing anything. There are plenty of free resources online as well as books to help you formulate an effective strategy. I've recommended some of those books at the back of this one.

- **Know your audience.**

This knowledge is foundational to any kind of communication or marketing. Where does your audience live, and how do they engage? Facebook? LinkedIn? Twitter? Google+? Tumblr? Blogs? You get the picture. This should give you some insight into where you ought to be active.

Social media is not just about getting people to where you are; it is also an opportunity to go to where your tribe dwells. Don't know where your friends are? Why not ask them? You'll be surprised to see how active they really are in these various platforms. Common   misperceptions such as, "Only young people are into social media" or "I don't have time to engage," are most definitely hindering many individuals and organizations from reaching their full potential.

- **It's not about online or offline.**

If you want to be an effective idea maker, you must understand the values that drive both online and offline credibility. The people I know who have a high level of credibility online also typically do a wonderful job of nurturing relationships offline. Whether it's through meet-ups, phone calls, or conferences, they stay accessible and never minimize the value of face-to-face engagement. There's still something about meeting in person that exponentially increases trust and credibility. More often than not, one's online world feeds the offline world and vice versa.

The reality today is that the line between online and offline are quickly blurring. For many, there isn't much of a practical distinction at all other than physicality. It's not that uncommon now for people to be meeting in person while communicating to each other via digital means.

"Need me to send you a reminder for the next meeting?"

"Yes, please."

"Great. I'll e-mail right now."

"Can you also send me that doc?"

"No problem. I'll just attach it to this reminder."

Sound familiar?

- **Don't forget the objectives!**

  It's still a best practice to first determine your objectives for using a medium. Even if you are not perfectly clear on your objectives before you start using an online tool, keep this need in mind as you explore the medium and articulate your objectives as you go. For example, how will you measure success for your online engagement?

  o Number of followers, friends, or fans?

  o Number of clicks on Facebook and Google ads?

  o Number of sales leads?

  o Return on investment for budget allocated to new media?

  o Growth of brand loyalty measured by surveys?

  o Collection of new data?

  o Research?

  o Community building?

  Determining objectives will help you set metrics, both qualitative and quantitative, so that you can determine how much success you're having online. Also, keep in mind that you don't have to use the same metrics for social media as you use for other marketing and communication platforms. Develop metrics that make sense for your company or organization. Like anything else you do, you should have a purpose behind why you participate and how you plan to measure impact.

- **Think empowerment, not control.**

  Social media is a powerful way to increase your brand presence and loyalty online. Nevertheless, those who seek to manage it in a big brother kind of way with their employees usually end up with little or no participation—and maybe even mutiny. Here's the general rule: dictatorships don't work. Remember, social media needs to be social; it must be relational.

  View social media as an opportunity to empower people in your company to live publicly in a way that betters their life and the life of the company. Individuals with strong personal brands usually do end up helping the company because those individual personal brands can lend credibility to an organization's efforts. Giving your staff freedom to engage social media both personally and professionally will heighten your effectiveness. If you are worried that people will spend time on their own social presence, you probably have to rethink who you're allowing on to the team and whether they're truly engaged in your mission.

- **Common sense wins out, so plan accordingly.**

Common sense isn't so common, is it? Common sense should tell you that all things online are public and, in most cases, embedded for eternity. It doesn't matter if you post something on a personal site. If it's visible at any point to the public, it's public and documented somewhere in cyberspace. In most cases, erasing the evidence won't guarantee that it's been removed.

Hopefully, this understanding is what guides your team's use of online media. Quite honestly, it's faulty thinking to think that we can separate our personal presence from our professional one online. They usually end up blending together. In other words, when it comes to social media, we're never off the clock. Your multiple worlds are now all connected.

I'm glad to see more and more industries strategically thinking through social media guidelines. For many workers, all that's required is to simply state the obvious and make them aware of the potential problems. Everyone can benefit from reminders of the obvious, especially if the obvious can prevent unnecessary job loss or company lawsuits.

- **Continue to learn and write.**

One of the most practical ways to get your idea out there is to consistently contribute thoughts to your field. This is where I think blogging is still a powerful platform for developing credibility for an idea. Unlike many other social media platforms, blogging allows you to archive, tag, and categorize your thoughts in a longer-lasting manner. Blogs are still far more searchable than Facebook, Twitter, or any other social media platform.

In addition, blogging allows you to gain credibility in a field. For example, if your idea is to introduce a new mobile product, I recommend that you regularly write about the world of mobile. Your posts don't always have to be about your specific product. In fact, you should have a nice mix of product updates as well as posts about the industry as a whole. Remember, you are a part of a greater tribe of people interested in your topic. Become a value-adder to your field. This will, in turn, give you more credibility and brand recognition.

Be sure to also write your thoughts in the form of comments or guest posts on other websites in your field. This usually creates new connections that provide further insights into your work. Reciprocal relationships are key to any endeavor.

Finally, stay patient. All of these things take time to develop. You don't just wake up one day with everyone wanting to hear about your new idea. Sharing your story in a digital world is not just about uploading your idea online. That part is quick and easy. If you want long-term impact and sustainable growth, you have to think more holistically. It's about building relationships both online and offline, allowing for organic growth through intentional strategy, and developing a clear sense of what you really want to do.

The good news is that we now have tools (many of which are free!) to get our story or idea out there in a way that was unfathomable just 10 years ago. Take time to explore our new digital world and leverage this unique opportunity. If you don't know how to do something online, do an Internet search. There's a good chance that you'll find a simple guide or a video that will show you how to get stuff done!

Good Idea (key thoughts from this section)	Now What? (your ideas and next steps for execution)
Getting a new idea out there looks a whole lot different today than it once did.	
Social media is not just about getting people to where you are, but also an opportunity to go to where your tribe dwells.	
Remember, social media needs to be social; it must be relational.	

Good Idea (key thoughts from this section)	Now What? (your ideas and next steps for execution)
One of the most practical ways to get your idea out there is to consistently contribute thoughts to your field.	_____ _____ _____

Taking It Further

- Think of your brand. Now quickly come up with 10 to 15 adjectives that describe it. Be honest and write the first things that come to mind. Don't overanalyze! Once you've done it, ask your team members to do this exercise as well. Now share your thoughts with one another and see if you are all on the same page. For further brand focusing, revisit the exercise suggestions in Chapter 37.
- When people think of you, what attributes do you believe they think of? Write down your thoughts and see if others agree with you.
- Get your pitch down in writing. Now go back over it and make it simpler and shorter. Turn it into an elevator pitch that could be delivered in just a couple of minutes. Make it memorable by incorporating all five senses. Now rehearse it with a family member or friend until you can deliver it comfortably.
- Where does your tribe dwell online? Facebook? Twitter? LinkedIn? If you don't know, reach out and ask them. Wherever they are is where you should focus your activity online.
- How will you measure success for your online presence? See the list in this chapter of possible metrics. Pick one or two and focus your team's activity on getting results in that area.
- Think of a blog topic that people in your field would benefit from reading and you would love to write about. Start that blog this week.

CONCLUSION

You made it!

(Or you cheated and jumped to this page!)

I hope this book has helped you move your ideas forward toward execution (as in implementation, not assassination—unless your ideas are bad and need to be put to rest).

As stated at the beginning of this book, the principles shared in *Good Idea. Now What?* came from the trenches of idea making and were designed to be extremely practical. This book was my attempt to articulate some of the wisdom I've gleaned over the years from thousands of idea makers who have consistently executed great ideas. I hope you have found several of these commonly practiced principles helpful in shaping your idea-making process.

As you continue to move ahead with your ideas, I'd like you to consider the following two foundational questions that may provide some guiding perspective for your life as an idea maker:

1. **What really matters?**

   I believe that life can be more fully enjoyed when we pursue things that really matter at the end of the day. Not all ideas are created equally. When it's all said and done, what will really matter in your life? Fame? Fortune? Family? Health? Legacy?

   In other words, are the ideas you are pursuing moving you in the direction of things that really matter to you? Keep in mind that each idea that is implemented well comes at a significant personal cost. There is no such thing as a free idea. Are the things you're giving up worth the potential return? If you can say "yes" to this question, then you should most definitely pursue your idea because it is a meaningful endeavor.

On the other hand, if you are simply distracted by a nicely dressed opportunity, I recommend that you pause and reflect on what it is you hope to ultimately accomplish through your new idea. Some ideas will be worth the sacrifice, whereas others will ultimately have little or no justification beyond the superficial.

Pursue things that really matter to you because things that matter provide a deep sense of purpose, pleasure, and peace.

2. What's enough?

This is certainly a difficult question to answer. On the surface, it may come off as limiting or restrictive, especially in a world that pushes us to a relentless pursuit of more. Why even bother to stop and determine how much is enough—whether we're talking about personal achievement or financial earning? Who cares? Isn't it our goal to get as much as we can?

Is it really?

The reason I ask you to consider this question is because without a good sense of what you're hoping to achieve and earn, there's a high probability that you'll lose sight of how much you ought to invest in your efforts. I've seen too many well-intentioned people give up way too much for things that in the end were simply not worth the investment of time and money that they made. Furthermore, some of these efforts came at the cost of losing irreplaceable time and irreparable relationships with family and friends. The level of commitment to an idea should have some correlation to what you hope to gain through the investment.

These two questions have really helped me determine which ideas I ought to pursue and how much effort should be dedicated to my endeavors.

A Note about Failure

Most idea makers I know struggle with the notion of failure. I think this is in part because most idea makers are high achievers and most achievers lean toward perfectionism and thus hate to fail at anything.

Failure, at some level, is inevitable for idea makers. Nevertheless, I am not a proponent of the thinking that says failure is essential to success.

In other words, don't go into a project expecting that failure has to be a part of the experience. Why would you start there?!

There's no doubt that we will all fail from time to time, but that's a far cry from those who expect to see it at every turn. Furthermore, failure is often relative to its context. For example, failure in the context of experimentation is more about refinement and proof of concept than it is about falling on one's face. Failing in this manner can actually point us more clearly to where we need to go. Failure often provides great direction toward success.

If we live with a perspective that says all ideas are imperfect and in development, it should relieve us of the false pressure of failure. All of our experiences, whether good or bad, can help create a pathway to success. If you're going to fail, fail forward!

We need you!

Your ideas matter.

Keep at it!

Don't just settle for being a lover of inspirational ideas. Rather, work hard toward implementing your concepts. Develop an infrastructure that allows your creativity to flourish and strategically collaborate with others to make your dream a reality. It's not impossible. It can be done. It must be done.

Our world needs you and will be a better place when your ideas come to life!

RECOMMENDATIONS FOR FURTHER READING

Idea Sparks

1. Gladwell, Malcolm. *Blink: The Power of Thinking without Thinking.* New York: Little, Brown and Co., 2007.
2. Gladwell, Malcolm. *Outliers: The Story of Success.* New York: Little, Brown and Co., 2008.
3. Godin, Seth. *Linchpin: Are You Indispensable?* New York: Portfolio, 2010.
4. Godin, Seth. *Poke the Box.* New York: Do You Zoom, 2011.
5. Griffin, W. Glenn. *The Creative Process Illustrated: How Advertising's Big Ideas Are Born.* Cincinnati: HOW Books, 2010.
6. Henry, Todd. *The Accidental Creative: How to Be Brilliant at a Moment's Notice.* New York: Portfolio/Penguin, 2011.
7. Johansson, Frans. *The Medici Effect: Breakthrough Insights at the Intersection of Ideas, Concepts, and Cultures.* Boston: Harvard Business School Press, 2004.
8. Johnson, Steven. *Where Good Ideas Come From: The Natural History of Innovation.* New York: Riverhead Books, 2010.
9. MacLeod, Hugh. *Ignore Everybody: And 39 Other Keys to Creativity.* New York: Portfolio, 2009.

Creative Process and Organization

1. Belsky, Scott. *Making Ideas Happen: Overcoming the Obstacles between Vision and Reality.* New York: Portfolio, 2010.

2. Fried, Jason, and David Heinemeier Hansson. *Rework*. New York: Crown Business, 2010.

3. Heath, Chip, and Dan Heath. *Made to Stick: Why Some Ideas Survive and Others Die*. New York: Random House, 2007.

4. Pressfield, Steven. *The War of Art: Break Through the Blocks and Win Your Inner Creative Battles*. New York: Warner Books, 2002.

Infrastructure and Strategy

1. Bossidy, Larry, and Ram Charan. *Execution: The Discipline of Getting Things Done*. New York: Crown Business, 2002.

2. Collins, Jim. *Good to Great: Why Some Companies Make the Leap . . . and Others Don't*. New York: HarperBusiness, 2001.

3. Gladwell, Malcolm. *The Tipping Point: How Little Things Can Make a Big Difference*. Boston: Back Bay Books, 2002.

4. Kiechel, Walter. *The Lords of Strategy: The Secret Intellectual History of the New Corporate World*. Boston: Harvard Business Press, 2010.

5. Osterwalder, Alexander, and Yves Pigneur. *Business Model Generation: A Handbook for Visionaries, Game Changers, and Challengers*. Hoboken, NJ: Wiley, 2010.

6. Pink, Daniel H. *Drive: The Surprising Truth about What Motivates Us*. New York: Riverhead Books, 2009.

7. Welch, Jack, with Suzy Welch. *Winning*. New York: Harper Business Publishers, 2005.

Collaboration and Tribes

1. Botsman, Rachel, and Roo Rogers. *What's Mine Is Yours: The Rise of Collaborative Consumption*. New York: Harper Business Publishers, 2010.

2. Godin, Seth. *Tribes: We Need You to Lead Us*. New York: Portfolio, 2008.

3. Hansen, Morten. *Collaboration: How Leaders Avoid the Traps, Create Unity, and Reap Big Results*. Boston: Harvard Business Press, 2009.

4. Logan, Dave. *Tribal Leadership: Leveraging Natural Groups to Build a Thriving Organization*. New York: Collins, 2008.

5. Rosen, Evan. *The Culture of Collaboration*. San Francisco: Red Ape, 2007.

Purpose

1. Hsieh, Tony. *Delivering Happiness: A Path to Profits, Passion, and Purpose*. New York: Business Plus, 2010.
2. Mycoskie, Blake. *Start Something That Matters*. New York: Spiegel & Grau, 2011.

New Media

1. Brogan, Chris, and Julien Smith. *Trust Agents: Using the Web to Build Influence, Improve Reputation, and Earn Trust*. Hoboken, NJ: Wiley, 2010.
2. Evans, Dave. *Social Media Marketing: The Next Generation of Business Engagement*. Indianapolis: Wiley, 2010.
3. Kanter, Beth, and Allison H. Fine. *The Networked Nonprofit: Connecting with Social Media to Drive Change*. San Francisco: Jossey-Bass, 2010.
4. Qualman, Erik. *Socialnomics: How Social Media Transforms the Way We Live and Do Business*. Hoboken, NJ: Wiley, 2011.
5. Safko, Lon, and David K. Brake. *The Social Media Bible: Tactics, Tools, and Strategies for Business Success*. Hoboken, NJ: Wiley, 2010.
6. Shirky, Clay. *Here Comes Everybody: The Power of Organizing without Organization*. New York: Penguin Press, 2008.
7. Vaynerchuk, Gary. *Crush It! Why NOW is the Time to Cash in on Your Passion*. New York: Harper Studio, 2009.

Brand/Marketing/Pitch

1. Harrison, Sam. *IdeaSelling: Successfully Pitch Your Creative Ideas to Bosses, Clients, & Other Decision Makers*. Cincinnati: HOW Books, 2010.
2. Kawasaki, Guy. *Enchantment: The Art of Changing Hearts, Minds, and Actions*. New York: Portfolio/Penguin, 2011.
3. Kawasaki, Guy. *Reality Check: The Irreverent Guide to Outsmarting, Outmanaging, and Outmarketing Your Competition*. New York: Portfolio, 2008.
4. Mainwaring, Simon. *We First: How Brands and Consumers Use Social Media to Build a Better World*. New York: Palgrave MacMillon, 2011.

This list is regularly being updated and expanded at www.GoodIdeaBook .com. Please visit for the latest additions.

ABOUT THE AUTHOR

Charles T. Lee is the chief executive officer (CEO) of Ideation (www .TheIdeation.com), an idea agency that specializes in helping businesses and organizations take their ideas and make them remarkable via creative strategy, branding, design, marketing, Web and social presence, and innovative events.

He is also a founding member of JustOne (www.Just4One.org), a nonprofit organization committed to creating "everyday ideas for human care." In addition, Charles is the creator of grassroots efforts including the Idea Camp, Ideation Conference, and the Freeze Project.

Charles regularly speaks on topics such as the creative process, idea making, innovation, branding, collaboration, new media, and compassionate justice. For details on Charles's speaking schedule, please visit www.CharlesTLee.com.

INDEX